THE GOURMET'S DIRECTORY

The Gourmet's Directory

Where to buy good food

Compiled by
Anne Beech

Illustrations by Dan Pearce

CROOM HELM LONDON

Croom Helm Ltd
2-10 St John's Road, London SW 11

ISBN: 0–85664–208–8

Printed and bound in Great Britain by
Redwood Burn Limited, Trowbridge & Esher

Introduction

Most of us spend a great deal of time thinking about food, buying it, preparing and consuming it. We are interested in food because we have to be and on the whole because we enjoy it. But good food is getting harder to find. And some foods — regional specialities, gourmet delicacies — are in danger of disappearing from all but a very few of our tables altogether, simply because we either don't know about them, or don't know where to find them.

Convenience foods have their place, certainly, in any well-stocked larder, and I would not suggest for a moment that we abandon them entirely and start again from scratch. Mass production, bulk buying, packaging and a national retail distribution have benefited all of us at one stage or another, and will probably continue to save us time and money in a good many cases. But as we are faced with an ever-diminishing choice between one highly technologised concoction and another (a roguishly cosmetic kipper, perhaps, or a pallid, sweating, tightly wrapped factory cheese), we begin to learn that the blessings are very mixed, that convenience foods are beginning to *replace* the better things in life, not enhance them. The large-scale processors and manufacturers have done us a great disservice: they have dictated choices to us, and they have changed and damaged the taste, the textures and the quality of our food in the process.

But at last the scales are starting to tip the other way. More and more of us are developing (or refining!) an interest in good food. Sadly, our new-found enthusiasms are all too often frustrated, as there is now an enormous gap between the consumer, anxious to experiment, revive old pleasures, try out alternatives, and the specialist supplier, driven out by the heavier retailing guns, who could meet those needs. The greengrocer who knows his produce and respects its season, the butcher, the fishmonger, and a host of other small retailers — the true specialists — are a rare species, elusive and very nearly extinct.

I hope that this directory will go some of the way towards bridging the gap between consumer and retailer by listing the sources, the suppliers, the specialists that survive, and by pointing out, in the introductions that preface each section, that the tastes and the foods that we enjoy now are part of a long and continuous history, a process to be appreciated and respected, and not lightly dismissed in the headlong rush towards standardisation.

As a first priority in compiling material for the directory, I have tried to locate specialist suppliers, within the various categories, who have the facilities to cater for a mail order trade — an increasingly large part of the 'gourmet' market. Specialist retailers who, for various reasons, deal only with personal shoppers have been included on the grounds that the service they offer is an exceptional one and could well justify a special journey.

Some foods, obviously, cannot be posted or delivered easily or economically. Where this is the case, I have tried to assemble a reasonably comprehensive list of suppliers throughout the country. The lists are not exhaustive. They would have made dull reading, and in many cases they would have been impossible or impractical to compile. Obviously, there are omissions and oversights and where this is so, I would beg indulgence. The book could have been extended into several volumes, and it would still have been incomplete.

Good food comes to us in many different guises, and although I have concentrated on sources of supply for the 'gourmet classics', I have also included what I feel are interesting alternatives – foods and beverages, some new, some very old and almost forgotten or only recently revived, that you may not have come across before. Armed with this directory, a little expertise and an enthusiasm for good food in any shape or form, the reader should be able to track down old favourites, experiment with new ideas and above all make use of the possibilities that exist before they disappear altogether.

I cannot begin to thank everyone who has helped me in the process of compiling material for this book. All of the contributors, most of them experts in their respective fields either as professionals or enthusiastic and knowledgeable amateurs, have earned my thanks and gratitude twice over. Their various introductions have greatly added to my own interest in the book, and I am quite sure that they will encourage the same enthusiasm on the part of the readers to find out more about the foods we eat, their histories, and their fascination. I would also like to thank Mr. Greenwood, at New Hall in Purleigh, for his hospitality and his patience in answering my questions; the Milk Marketing Board; the Scotch Whisky Association; the White Fish Authority and the Herring Industry Board; and the countless others who have been pestered and interrogated over a period of months. Without their help and their knowledge, the entire project would have been an impossibility, and I wish I could name them all. One particular thank you goes to David Croom, who was probably annoyed and worried but didn't show it, and to James Atkinson, who only just survived.

Dairy Produce

CHEESE: A BRIEF HISTORY

A. McEwan

Cheese is the most all-purpose food we have. Its character and uses can be so varied that we have to look beyond cheese itself for the reasons why different peoples have developed quite unrelated cheese-eating habits.

The first cheese originated in the Neolithic Age, in ancient Egypt and among the pastoral tribes of the biblical Middle East. They were only separated sour milk curds, made when cow, ewe or nanny-goat was milked into a none-too-clean goatskin bag. These peoples soon learned to press the curds to drain off the whey and make compact, dryish curd 'cakes' of varying degrees of hardness. Who would not prefer to carry on his saddle or his back a firm, small lump of concentrated food instead of a bulging goatskin full of slops? They made cottage-style, mostly unsalted, unripened cheeses which had to be eaten within hours of being made.

Throughout the Middle East today the women still make these cheeses, which, with yogurts, are a first-class substitute for the cream, eggs and butter of countries where pasture replaces desert sands or steep bare hills. They use them a great deal in their *mezze* or *hors d'oeuvre*, and also in a variety of large and small savoury and sweet pies and cheese-cakes, eaten both between and at meals. These dishes are an important element in the long social interchanges which are part of their laws of etiquette.

In Greece, a rocky land of thin soil, cheese has also played a vital part in the diet, as well as in social relations, since earliest times. It still does so. Outside every village food shop hangs a bag of the goat's or ewe's curd cheese called *myzithra*; and in southern Greece the table is not considered set until this unsalted myzithra (or the better known salty *feta*) cheese is on it, to be sprinkled or spread on any and every dish. It is an essential ingredient, for instance, of the standard salad *paysanne* eaten every day – a habit derived from earlier times when most Greeks saw little or no meat protein.

It was people like these who, in ancient times, first learned how to encourage souring in milk by adding thistles and other herbs, and then how to 'start' their own curds using rennet – a discovery probably made by finding milk curds in a calf's stomach after slaughtering it. 'Started' curds were more pleasant to the taste than soured curds. More important, they also lasted better. The enzymes in the curds would work on them for a long time, so they could be ripened. Thus, in lands which carried cattle, semi-hard and hard cheeses in all their variety could now be made from rich summer milk and stored for winter when most of the cattle had been killed off.

The Romans were the first to write about these cheeses. They made a lot of them, most of them salted or brined or smoked, and their soldiers carried hunks of them as military rations. Ordinary folk also used them, sliced raw into salads or cooked in various sweet or savoury pastry and other dishes. They do not seem to have had any special place in the menu. The Romans introduced their cheese, like so much else, everywhere they went in Europe. England was then, as now, one of the prime dairying countries and a lot of cheese was probably eaten. Pottery cheese-wrings have been found on many Romano-British sites.

England was a richly timbered land, and sea-girt. Her climate was mild, her soil kindly. So her invaders soon became settlers. These facts seem to have dictated why she first developed different uses for cheese, different types, and different times for eating cheese from her European neighbours.

After the Norse and Norman invasions, there were two main types of Englishman: Anglo-Saxon and Celts. The Anglo-Saxons were mainly sheep-rearers, so the cheeses in their areas were made mostly from ewe's milk until at least the seventeenth century. The ewe's milk cheeses were, generally, milder, cleaner and richer and were produced more easily than the ones made from cow's milk, which were the 'white meats' of the Celts who had always been cattle breeders. At first these peoples, divided into tribes, all lived in much the same way whether they were rich or poor, chieftains or serfs. Food was scarce for everyone, especially in winter, so cheese was a food valued by any man when hunting failed; although between whiles it was eaten more by children and invalids than by strong men, who preferred red meat.

But with time social differences crept in between rich and poor, and with them different foods for different classes of people. From early medieval times onwards, full-milk and cream-enriched cheeses were made virtually only for wealthy men, who also ate a good deal of cream. So the dairy of a manoral lord, or a great abbey, usually had more skimmed milk and buttermilk than the household could use. This was given to the labourers and peasants, or was made into hard-skim-milk cheeses for them.

The wealthy, who preferred flesh meats, fresh in summer, preserved in winter, kept their softer, creamier 'white meats' for custards, cheese-cakes, sweet dishes and sauces.

The peasants, on the whole, could not keep stocks of smoked or salted meat for winter use. But the hard cheeses improved with storage and could be used in winter when even rabbits and wild birds were often scarce. So naturally the peasant ate a great deal of cheese, made both from his own cow's buttermilk and from the products his master gave him. It became his staple protein food.

He used it in various ways. For instance, it was his standard meal when in the fields, and at harvest time hard cheese was sometimes specially bought to feed the extra farm workers. After work he ate cheese with a primitive kind of pasta, used it to supplement his meagre meat, mixed it with eggs or herbs or toasted it (especially in Wales).

It did him no harm. But his master had come to believe that hard cheese was bad for any sufferer from wind, especially at night — though his own indigestion was usually due to an over-rich dinner. He therefore only ate a little after dinner or at his late-night supper to 'close his stomach' — its fat was thought to lie on top of the food and seal it in the stomach, like an oil layer. Here, already, we see the lines of English cheese-eating habits through the centuries being laid down: the use of cheese in high tea or early supper dishes, or right at the end of a more elaborate meal.

Several factors fixed these habits in the English way of eating. One was the pudding. Because her people had unlimited timber for fuel, and fine corn land too, England made one unique contribution to western cookery. Her 'boyled', or rather simmered, one-pot meal of broth, bones, meat and vegetables had come to include a starchy pudding boiled in a cloth bag. At first it was a plain dough eaten with or after the broth as a filler before one ate the meat; only later were meat, fruit, spices and sugar all mixed into the pudding itself, and only much later still was it refined into the sweet boiled pudding.

The farm worker, and later the industrial worker, who ate his main hot meal soon after he got home from work, ate his cheese with his meat after his 'pudden filler'; and he went on eating his cheese after his pudding even when it became a sweet one.

Another significant factor was the timing of meals. In medieval Europe, the rich man's dinner was served between 3 and 4 o'clock in the afternoon, and a 'livery' or snack cupboard-meal was taken in one's room shortly before bed-time. The often riotously rich dinner did not include cheese save in sweet cheese-cakes, since wealthy Englishmen had developed contempt for plain cheese as a plebeian taste. But the late-night snack supper often did, since it was convenient cupboard food as well as the classic way to 'close' the stomach.

Over the centuries the dinner hour became later and later; and in time dinner and supper were often run together, so that the late-night cheese snack got tagged on to the end of the dinner — where it remained. Since the English class system was more fluid than the Continental ones, the men of wealth and power often had plebeian origins; they might be snobs but were not so foolish as to refuse the good plain cheeses of their earlier days. The status of cheese rose.

Much more important, however, in giving cheese a defined place was the English delight in wine. In medieval times, English demand for claret had created and maintained the great Bordeaux vineyards as we know them. In the Napoleonic Wars when French wines were unobtainable, Englishmen created the Spanish and Portuguese wines. Englishmen drank wine at any time, but sustained drinking, especially of claret, was carried on from dinner time onward. The English cheeses were by nature the perfect complement to these after-dinner wines, and so naturally took their place at the end of the dinner to accompany them.

To the French this habit must have seemed barbarous. They had hundreds of different, subtle, soft and firm cheeses, most of them fitted by their flavour to be a course on their own in any dinner, and they had wines for every mood and moment. They drank at any time of the day, not concentratedly in the evenings. Then, too, the French were always close followers of the menu pattern of the Italians, for whom cheese was still an important savoury meat substitute among all classes.

Naturally, then, the French kept their cheeses in the savoury section of their dinner, using them principally to cleanse their palates, as a course to finish the red wine with or to introduce a sweeter white, and sometimes as the sole protein, for example in Lenten fare.

For the Scandinavians, Germans and Dutch, the situation was different. The Catholic faith had always sat more lightly on them, but the rigours of their climate did not. The sea was ever-present, ever-threatening. So was the cold. One great merit of cheese for them was that it need not be as heavily salted as fish to be a good winter preserve – possibly one reason for their bland cheeses. They must always have made a good deal of cheese even in the days when much of their soil was sour and salt. For, like all Anglo-Saxons (including the English), they probably kept more sheep than cattle then, and made mostly ewe's milk cheeses, as mountain peoples still do. Sheep grazed readily enough on salt-marsh grass.

These northern lands grew far fewer fresh herbs than the south (another reason for their mild-flavoured cheeses), and had a much shorter summer season. Hens did not lay in the long, snow-bound winter, so eggs were few. Yet these people liked to eat large solid meals against the cold; also they had a mercantile streak which made them value material things in quantity as well as quality.

Since cheese was a pleasantly mild change from salt fish, solid and always at hand even when eggs were not, what could be more natural than to keep to the custom of eating it for breakfast, even after the wealthy in countries like England and Norman France had abandoned the steak, cheese and beer breakfast of medieval times? They still do so.

We must not underestimate this power of custom in maintaining food habits. The modern cheese-eating habits of the Middle Eastern peoples and the Greeks have their roots far back in their food-scarce history. Roman Catholic areas still give cheese a vital place among their savoury foods. They have not relegated it to a subsidiary meal or to the end of the main meal.

Inland and in mountain areas, where poor people cannot feed themselves on fish, they use cheese as an important savoury food in their main meals. Hence the use in many dishes of the savoury goat's cheeses of the Spanish and Mexican highlands, the value set by Italians on Dolcelatte and Gorgonzola, and the pride local people take in the herb and garlic-flavoured cheeses of the mountain regions of France.

Cheese is still, as it always has been, the poor man' staple diet. The wealthy have always tended to scorn it as 'peasant fare'; and often none more so than the newly-rich merchants of each period in the northern Protestant Republics, who needed to establish themselves as a superior class. People like these have had a marked influence in keeping cheese as a breakfast dish or as a snack in their households. Only recently has cheese overcome this centuries-old outlook; either because it has become socially useful or a money-spinning export.

Another factor in maintaining cheese-eating habits is what people are accustomed to drink. For 300 years (from 1142-53 when the English owned Bordeaux), they drank more 'clairet' and 'Clarret' than anyone else in Europe. Since their custom, derived from their Anglo-Saxon ancestors, was to drink largely after dinner, that was when they ate their cheese too. When, later, due to the Napoleonic Wars, they changed to port, sherry and Madeira, these wines were, again, for after-dinner drinking – usually with cheese. So we have clung to this place for our cheese, although coffee has replaced the wines of former days.

Only in the late nineteenth century, when champagne became virtually the only wine drunk by society at meals, did cheese lose its importance, and it was then hardly ever served at any upper- or middle-class dinner.

It has returned now for three good reasons. First, a great many of us are protein-conscious slimmers. Second, few of us can afford to drink great wines, or both dry and sweet wines, or after-dinner brandy. So we tend to drink more plebeian and young wines with our meals, and sometimes afterwards. Third, we are not only less rich, we are less formal than we used to be; and we find in wine and cheese and similar parties a relaxed, useful and pleasant way to entertain.

SOURCES OF SUPPLY

Cheese suppliers have been divided into three sections, for convenience: shops and stores; mail order suppliers; and a separate section for specialist retailers in London.

Shops and Stores

With the exception of the larger general grocery stores, as far as possible, I have included in the list below only those highly specialised stores which concentrate on stocking an exceptionally wide range of British farmhouse cheeses and Continental cheeses.

BERKSHIRE

Wells Stores, Streatley-on-Thames (prop: P. Vance)
One of the best-known of the cheese specialists outside London. Enormous range of cheeses, some of which can be sent by post. Occasionally stocks the elusive Blue Vinny, probably the rarest of the English cheeses.

CORNWALL

Folley and Sons of the Castle Stores, Launceston, Cornwall.
Tel: Launceston 2065.

Wonnacotts Dairy, 4 Lansdown Road, Bude, Cornwall. Tel: Bude 3105.
Farmhouse cheese specialists.

ESSEX

P. Burton, Burton of Chelmsford, 16 Broomfield Road, Chelmsford.

HAMPSHIRE

Mr. Woodman, Woodman's (Fleet) Ltd., 150-156 Aldershot Road, Fleet.
Tel: 3637.

Robert Jacksons 37-41 Seamoor Road, Bournemouth.
Tel: Bournemouth 61361.

HERTFORDSHIRE

Marriden's Stores, 5 High Street, Harpenden.

Robert Jacksons, 9 George Street, St. Albans. Tel: St. Albans 63774.

Robert Jacksons, Halsey and Sons, Market Place, Hitchin. Tel: Hitchin 2023

KENT

Dartford Health Food Centre, 86 Dartford Road, Dartford. Tel: Dartford 23578.
Despite the name, the shop does stock an exceptionally wide range of English and Continental cheeses, in addition to the more predictable health food items.

Robert Jacksons, 37 Mount Ephraim, Tunbridge Wells.
Tel: Tunbridge Wells 20342.

LINCOLNSHIRE

W. Carrotte, 51 Lord Street, Gainsborough.

SURREY

F. G. Hawkes, 190 Green Lane, Shepperton.

S. Andrews, 20 Cross Road, Tadworth. Tel: Tadworth 2125.

W. G. Reeves, 8 The Broadway, Woking. Tel: Woking 61629.

SUSSEX

Clough and Sons, 27-31 Sunte Avenue, Lindfield, Haywards Heath.
Tel: Haywards Heath 52060.

WARWICKSHIRE

Russell Gorman, Erdington Market, Barnabus Road, Erdington, Birmingham 23.
Tel: 021 373 1862.

WILTSHIRE

Marlborough Delicatessen, 9 London Road, Marlborough.
Tel: Marlborough 2877.

WORCESTERSHIRE

Russell Gorman, 475 Bearwood Road, Smethwick. Tel: 021 429 1100.

YORKSHIRE

T. A. and G. Wood, 52 Cleasby Road, Menston, Ilkley LS29 6HT.

J. V. Milton, Standings, Harrogate.

C. E. Baggs and Sons Ltd., 6-8 Toll Gavel, Beverley.

SCOTLAND

Jas. Ferguson and Co., Union Street, Glasgow.

Choosa Cheese, 178 Bruntsfield Place, Edinburgh.

McDonald's, Buchanan Street, Glasgow.

The Lairds Larder, 36 Victoria Street, Edinburgh. Tel: 031 226 5519.

Mail Order Suppliers

Danfood Ltd., 37 Raynham Road, Industrial Estate, Bishops Stortford, Herts.
Tel: 0279 56399.

As the name suggests, specialist suppliers of Danish foods. Danablu, Danbo (with caraway seeds), Esrom, Fynbo, Havarti, Samsø, and Maribo, all available by post.

Grants, High Street, Croydon. Tel: 01 688 4400.
Stiltons only, during the Christmas period.

Grays of Worcester Ltd., Orchard Street, Worcester WR5 3DP.
Tel: 0905 352388.
No orders by phone. Stiltons only.

Gifthams, The Quadrant, Hoylake, Wirral, Cheshire L47 2EE. Tel: 051 632 3194.
Farmhouse Cheshire (4 lb. miniature), or pack containing Cheshire and 1 lb. Stilton. Orders cannot be dispatched to addresses in Northern Ireland or Eire.

Paxton and Whitfield, 93 Jermyn Street, London SW1Y 6JE. Tel: 01 930 3380.
At Christmas and throughout the year, a few cheeses are available by mail order: Truckle and small Truckle Cheddar, Blue Cheshire, Red Cheshire, Stilton (packed in stoneware jars or sold as small, medium or large individual cheeses), Baby Stilton. All subject to availability (see also London Specialist Stores, below).

Young and Saunders Ltd., 5 Queensferry Street, Edinburgh EH2 4PD.
Tel: 031 225 6075.
Postal service and deliveries: daily within Edinburgh, weekly to the Lothians, Central Fife; fortnightly to most of the Border counties. Also open to personal shoppers. Vast range of English and Continental cheeses, including whole Stiltons, Blue Cheshire, Red Cheshire, Derbyshire Sage, Lancashire, White Wensleydale, Farmhouse Cheddar, Caerphilly, over twenty French cheeses and a representative selection of Swiss, German, Norwegian, Italian, Dutch, Danish and Austrian cheeses. They also offer a number of Scottish cheeses: Orkney Farmhouse, Blarlaith Crowdie, Caboc, Arran Dunlop, Ayrshire Cream and Islay.

London Specialist Stores

Camisa and Son, 61 Old Compton Street, London W1N 5PN. Tel: 01 437 7610.
Italian cheeses: Parmesan (block, sometimes difficult to find), Provolone, Gorgonzola, Dolcelatte, Mozzarella.

Danish Food Centre, 2-3 Conduit Street, London W1. Tel: 01 499 7040.
As the name implies, Danish cheeses. (NB: there are also Danish Food Centres at the following addresses throughout the UK: Cross Street, Manchester 2; 10 Stephenson Place, Birmingham; 48 Vincent Street, Glasgow.)

Fortnum and Masons, 184 Piccadilly, London W1. Tel: 01 734 8040.
An almost complete range of the finest English cheeses – Stiltons, Cheddars, Cheshires, Leicester, Derby, Wensleydale, Caerphilly, etc. Also have occasional

stocks of the rare (and expensive) Canadian Black Diamond Cheddar.

German Food Centre, 44 Knightsbridge, London SW1. Tel: 01 235 5760.
Fairly expensive range of German cheeses.

Harrods, Brompton Road, London SW1. Tel: 01 730 1234.
English and Continental cheeses, a wide variety of both and all excellent quality.

Jacksons, 171 Piccadilly, London W1. Tel: 01 493 1033.
Also branches at 6a and b Sloane Street, SW1; and 24 Kendal Street, W2.
Good selection of mostly English cheeses.

Justin de Blank, 42 Elizabeth Street, London SW1. Tel: 01 750 0605.
Also at 136 Brompton Road, SW3 (Tel: 01 584 8144); and 54 Duke Street, W1 (Tel: 01 629 3174).
Small selection of British farmhouse cheeses and a range of French cheeses.

Le Cochon Rose, 83 Lower Sloane Street, London SW1. Tel: 01 730 0605.
Basic range of French cheeses.

Parmigiano Figlio, 43 Frith Street, London W1. Tel: 01 437 4728.
Wide range of Italian cheeses, including (occasionally) block Parmesan.

Paxton and Whitfield, 93 Jermyn Street, London SW1. Tel: 01 930 3380.
The doyen of London's cheese retailers. Over 80 cheeses in stock, both English and Continental. Various grades and sizes of Cheddar and Cheshire (blue and red), Gloucester, Sage Derby, Wensleydale (white and blue), Windsor red (a fairly recent innovation, first introduced nine years ago), and of course Stilton. An enormous range of French cheeses includes the elusive Vacherin, difficult to locate in France, let alone England.

Shores, 413 Kings Road, SW6. Tel: 01 352 4545.
Fairly standard range of English and Continental cheeses, but placed in the specialist class as they occasionally stock Blue Vinny.

Swiss Centre, Leicester Square, London W2. Tel: 01 734 1291.
The Gourmet Corner in the centre carries a range of Swiss delicacies, including all the Swiss cheeses available in this country.

EGGS

The debate over free-range eggs versus battery-produced eggs and poultry has gone on for some time. A good many cookery writers (and nutritionists, come to that) still prefer to use free-range eggs whenever possible, and a mass of available evidence suggests that there might be something in the claim that free-range eggs are more nutritious and flavoursome.

With the recent increase in the cost of battery eggs, price is no longer quite the obstacle it once was, but there remains the problem of availability. It has been estimated that only 4 per cent of total egg production in the UK is from free-range birds, and there is no national marketing operation for free-range eggs. And even if you can track them down, there are no guarantees that eggs sold as free-range are what they claim to be. The Farm and Food Society have pointed out on more than one occasion that there is probably more fraudulent trading in eggs than in any other branch of food production.

If you are not interested in using free-range eggs, then this section will be of little use to you. But for those of you who think that there might be something in those claims for extra flavour, better taste and better (relative) value, the following list of shops and stores throughout the UK will hopefully be of some use. A word of warning: only those stores marked with an asterisk produce or sell eggs that are absolutely guaranteed as free-range. They are the concerns that have been inspected and approved by the Farm and Food Society, whose primary objectives are to restore the principles of sound farming techniques and the production of good food. The remaining stores are likely to have free-range eggs, and probably do. But verbal promises are worth next to nothing, and you will simply have to use your judgement.

SOURCES OF SUPPLY

With the exception of the Greater London area, which appears at the end of the listings, the following are arranged county by county, with separate listings for Scotland and Wales.

ENGLAND

BERKSHIRE

Health Stores, 19 West Saint Helen Street, Abingdon-on-Thames.

E. P. Spackman, Market Place, Hungerford.

Country Market Health Foods, 122 High Street, Maidenhead.

A. W. Luff, 17 The Broadway, Newbury.

Country Fare, 29 St. Leonards Road, Windsor.

BUCKINGHAMSHIRE

Amersham Health Foods, 156 Station Road, Amersham.

Delikatesserie, 56 Kingsbury, Aylesbury.

Springhill Farm, Dinton, nr. Aylesbury (Farm, Tel: Aylesbury 432).*

Nashleigh Hill Nurseries, 20 Red Lion Street, Chesham.

Real Foods, 6 The Arcade, Octagon Precinct, High Wycombe.

CHESHIRE

Health Food Centre, 41 Oxford Road, Altrincham.

Henry's Dairy, Whitfield Buildings, Pensby Road, Heswall, Wirral.

Duttons, Godstall Lane, Off Eastgate Street, Chester.

Vital Foods, Church Street, Wilmslow.

CORNWALL

Honey and Health Food Centre, 5 Honey Street, Bodmin.

Harbour Lights, 51 Fore Street, Newquay.

Wonnacotts Dairy, 4 Lansdown Road, Bude.

S. Piper and Sons, 1 Francis Street, Truro.

Troy Dairy, 10 Lostwithiel Street, Fowey.

Chapman's Dairy, Trevanson Street, Wadebridge.

COUNTY DURHAM

The Health Food Centre, 4a Bondgate, Bishop Auckland.

DEVON

Healthwise Health Foods, Lyme Street, Axminster.

Health Food Stores, 14a Bridgland Street, Bideford.

Chilcotts Dairy, 16 Litchdon Street, Barnstaple.

Crook's Stores, 5 High Street, Crediton.

Cranks, 13 Foss Street, Dartmouth.

The Herb Shop, 1 Angel Terrace, Tiverton.

Health Foods, 13 Brook Street, Tavistock.

The Herb of Grace, Butterwalk, Totnes.

DORSET

Blandford Health Foods, 43a East Street, Blandford Forum.

Swanage Bay Stores, 12 Redcliffe Road, Swanage.

Lowman's Stores, 2 Wyke Street, Gillingham.

ESSEX

Buckhurst Hill Health Stores, 24 Queens Road, Buckhurst Hill.

H. Gunton, 81/83 Crouch Street, Colchester.

Liddard, Broadly Common, nr. Harrow.

Loughton Health Stores, 285 High Road, Loughton.

Woodford Health Stores, 83 High Road, Woodford.

GLOUCESTERSHIRE

The Old Bakehouse, 3 Sherborne Street, Bourton-on-the-Water.

HAMPSHIRE

Health Foods, 4 The Triangle, Bournemouth.

P. D. Emery, 8 New Road Junction, Northbourne, Bournemouth.

The Mascot Stores, Seafield Road, Isle of Wight.

HERTFORDSHIRE

Health Food Store, 198 High Street, Berkhampstead.

KENT

Health Foods, 403 Croydon Road, Beckenham.

Chiesman's, High Street, Maidstone.

Spice of Life, 87 Station Road, Birchington, Margate.

The Fruit Shop, 26 London Road, Sevenoaks.

Lowe's of Canterbury, 21 The Borough, Canterbury.

Chiesman's, Calverley Road, Tunbridge Wells.

Deva Wholefoods, 12 Church Street, Folkestone.

LANCASHIRE

The Circle Health Food Centre, 311 Dickson Road, Blackpool.

Davies, 175 Duke Street, St. Helens.

Finer Food, 613a Wilbraham Road, Chorlton-cum-Hardy, Manchester 21.

J. and M. Slater, 53 Halifax Road, Todmorden.

Beels Pure Foods, 36 Yorkshire Street, Morecambe.

LINCOLNSHIRE

J. W. Field and Son, 18 Holl Place, Spalding.

MIDDLESEX

Ashford Health Store, 10 Station Road, Ashford.

Realfoods, 3/5 Station Road, Edgware.

Country Market Stores, 22 High Street, Ruislip.

Countryfare, 29 Church Road, Stanmore.

NORFOLK

Norwich Health Food Stores, 8 White Lion Street, Norwich.

Taylor's Herbs and Wholefoods, 15 Lower Goat Lane, Norwich.

OXFORDSHIRE

S. Savins and Son, 92 Sheep Street, Bicester.

Wholefoods, 6 Suffolk House, Banbury Road, Summertown, Oxford.

STAFFORDSHIRE

Friar Tuck Delicatessen, 11a Church Street, Tamworth.

SOMERSET

Realfoods, 6 Cheap Street, Bath.

Harrison's Health Stores, 3 Binford Place, Bridgwater.

Manor Farm Dairy, 259 Gloucester Road, Bishopston, Bristol.

Boddy's Limited, 42 High Street, Taunton.

Weston Health Food Centre, 7 Magdala Buildings, Weston-super-Mare.

Andrew W. Kerr's, 33 Southwalk, The Shopping Centre, Yate, nr. Bristol.

SUFFOLK

Marno's Food Reform Shop, 14 St. Nicholas Street, Ipswich.

Faulkner's Delicatessen, 1 Golden Court, Bridge Road, Oulton Broad.

Rendham Stores, Rendham, Saxmundham.

Henry's, 1 Thoroughfare, Woodbridge.

SURREY

F. Stokes and Sons Ltd., 38 Park Street, Camberley.

Country Market Health Foods, 3 Chipstead Valley Road, Coulsdon.

The Pure Food Company, 100 High Street, Croydon.

Realfoods, 185 High Street, Dorking.

Loseley Farm Shop, Crown Court, 44 High Street, Godalming.

Cranks Health Shop, 35 Castle Street, Guildford.

Loseley House Shop, Guildford.

Leatherhead Wholefood Shop, 34 High Street, Leatherhead.

W. A. Carpenter, Ockley Provision Stores, Ockley.

Realfoods, 11 Church Path, Woking.

SUSSEX

Nature's Way, 64 Devonshire Road, Bexhill-on-Sea.

Ceres Health Foods, 3/5 Bolton Road, Eastbourne.

The Seasons, Lewes Road, Forest Row.

Michaels Stores, Main Road, Middleton-on-Sea, Bognor Regis.

Spice of Life, 16a Fair Lane, Robertsbridge.

St. Leonards Wholefoods, 45c London Road, St. Leonards-on-Sea.

M. Pitkethly Health Stores, 4 Becket Buildings, Littlehampton Road, Worthing.

WARWICKSHIRE

Wholefood and Home Brew, 59 Mill Street, Bedworth.

Prana Wholefoods Ltd., 20 Priory Ringway, Birmingham 4.*

Prana Wholefoods Ltd., 15 Central Square, Erdington, Birmingham 23.*

Prana Wholefoods Ltd., 95 High Street, Harborne, Birmingham 17.*

Country Market Health Foods, 44 The Square, Kenilworth.

Prana Wholefoods Ltd., 33 Alcester Road, King's Heath, Birmingham 14.*

Prana Wholefoods Ltd., 22 Grosvenor Shopping Centre, Northfield, Birmingham 31.*

Prana Wholefoods Ltd., 14 Drury Lane, Solihull.*

R. E. Maxwell, 5 Tiddington Road, Stratford-on-Avon.

Prana Wholefoods Ltd., 20 Birmingham Road, Sutton Coldfield.*

Prana Wholefoods Ltd., Sandwell Shopping Centre, West Bromwich.*

WESTMORLAND

The Cornershop, Windermere, Crescent Road.

WILTSHIRE

Marlborough Delicatessen, 9 London Road, Marlborough.

Rose and Sons, 29 Bond Street, Trowbridge.

WORCESTERSHIRE

Prana Wholefoods Ltd., 80 High Street, Bromsgrove.*

Prana Wholefoods Ltd., 6 High Street, Droitwich.*

Prana Wholefoods Ltd., 21 Precinct, Halesowen.*

Health and Speciality Foods, 65 Church Street, Malvern.

Prana Wholefoods Ltd., 8 Evesham Street, Redditch.*

Prana Wholefoods Ltd., 59 High Street, Stourbridge.*

YORKSHIRE

G. Jack and Sons, 6 Wednesday Market, Beverley.

Grain, 33 Princes Avenue, Hull.

Realfoods, 11 Arndale Centre, Crossgate, Leeds.

The Sunshine Shops, Orchard Street, Sheffield 1.

N. and D. Whiting, 69 Bootham, York.

York Wholefood, 98 Micklegate, York.

WALES

CAERNARVONSHIRE

H. Pugh Jones, 50 High Street, Criccieth.

CARDIGANSHIRE

Rylands Health Centre, 28 Chalybeate Street, Aberystwyth.

E. N. and F. R. Picton, Delicatessen, 55 Prendre, Cardigan.

Stafford House Shop, Llandysull.

CARMARTHENSHIRE

Primrose Health Food and Herbal Stores, 30 Quay Street, Ammanford.

Waverley Stores Ltd., 23 Lammas Street, Carmarthen.

DENBIGHSHIRE

Duttons Sigarro Stores, 1 High Street, Wrexham.

GLAMORGAN

Quadrille Health Store, 77 Pontcanna Street, Cathedral Road, Cardiff.

Mumbles Health Fayre, 622 Mumbles Road, Southend, Swansea.

PEMBROKESHIRE

Fedwen Stores, Efailwen, Clynderwen.

SCOTLAND

DUNBARTONSHIRE

A. Bulloch and Co., 32 West Clyde Street, Helensburgh.

LANARKSHIRE

Airdrie Health Foods, 174 Clark Street, Airdrie.

MIDLOTHIAN

Henderson's Farm Shop, 92 Hanover Street, Edinburgh.

The Health Food Shop, 37 West Port, Arbroath, Angus.

London Stores Stocking Free-Range Eggs

The stores listed below have all been approved by the Farm and Food Society inspectors, and bear their seal of approval.

Wholefood, 112 Baker Street, London W1.

Cranks, 8 Marshall Street, London W1.

Brownies, 36 Rosslyn Hill, London NW3.

Kirry, 196 Haverstock Hill, London NW3.

The Garden Centre, 788 Finchley Road, London NW11.

Wholesome Fare, Kensington High Street, London W8.

Barkers, Kensington High Street, London W8.

Harrods, Knightsbridge, London SW7.

Moores, Sloane Street, London SW1.

Robert Jacksons, Sloane Street, London SW1.

Kensington Delicatessen, 166 Brompton Road, London SW7.

R. V. Delicatessen, 113 Wandsworth High Street, London SW18.

Osmonds, Lower Richmond Road, London SW14.

Jones, 36 Barnes High Street, London SW13.

Parkfield, 297 Upper Richmond Road, London SW15.

Pyx Good Food, Station Buildings, Coombe Lane, Raynes Park, London SW20.

Health Foods, 324 Bethnal Green Road, London E2.

Vann's Health Centre, 28 Kirkdale Road, Leytonstone.

CREAM

Eleven different types of cream are usually produced, ranging from pasteurised single cream to sterilised half cream to the richest of them all — farmhouse clotted cream. For the purposes of this book, I have concentrated on sources of supply for the latter.

Cornish clotted cream is said to be 'nuttier' than its Devon counterpart, but both are made in the same way: the milk is heated to a temperature of about 82°C (180°F) and left to cool for four and a half hours. The 'crust' that forms during that time is then skimmed off and packed into cartons by hand. As the cream itself is exceptionally thick, postage and packing present no real problems — and if you are not in the habit of paying regular visits to the south west, 'cream by post' is a perfectly reasonable way of buying it, unless you can be sure that the clotted cream available in a local store is the real thing, and not a barely acceptable substitute, which it often is.

SOURCES OF SUPPLY

I have listed a number of dairies and other concerns who are able to take postal orders for clotted cream — usually in ½ lb. or 1 lb. quantities. In some cases, the cream by post trade is a seasonal one, and supplies cannot be guaranteed throughout the year.

Grays of Worcester Ltd., Orchard Street, Worcester WR5 3DP.
(Christmas period only)

Babbacombe Creamery, 124 Reddenhill Road, Babbacombe, Torquay, Devon.

Courtlands Products Ltd., Courtlands Cross, Exmouth, Devon.

Express Dairies (Western), Salterton Road, Exmouth, Devon.

Penzance Buttery (Cream Office), Alverton, Penzance, Cornwall.

Wonnacotts Dairy, 4 Lansdown Road, Bude, Cornwall.

Cream by post is also available from the following branches of the Plymouth and South Devon Co-operative Society:

The Food Hall, Plymouth and South Devon Co-operative Soc., Raleigh Street,

Plymouth PL1 1ET.

Tor House Food Hall, 77/79 Union Street, Torquay, Devon.

Tavistock Central Co-op, Market Street, Bank Square, Tavistock PL19 0DE.

Brixham Central Co-op, 75 Fore Street, Brixham, Devon.

Paignton Central Co-op, Winner Street, Paignton TQ3 3EW.

Buckfastleigh Central Co-op, 33 Chapel Street, Buckfastleigh, Devon.

Newton Abbot Central Co-op, 17 Queen Street, Newton Abbot, Devon.

Moretonhampstead Co-op, Court Street, Moretonhampstead, Devon TQ13 8NE.

Bovey Tracey Co-op, 42 Fore Street, Bovey Tracey TQ13 9AD.

Game, Meat and Poultry

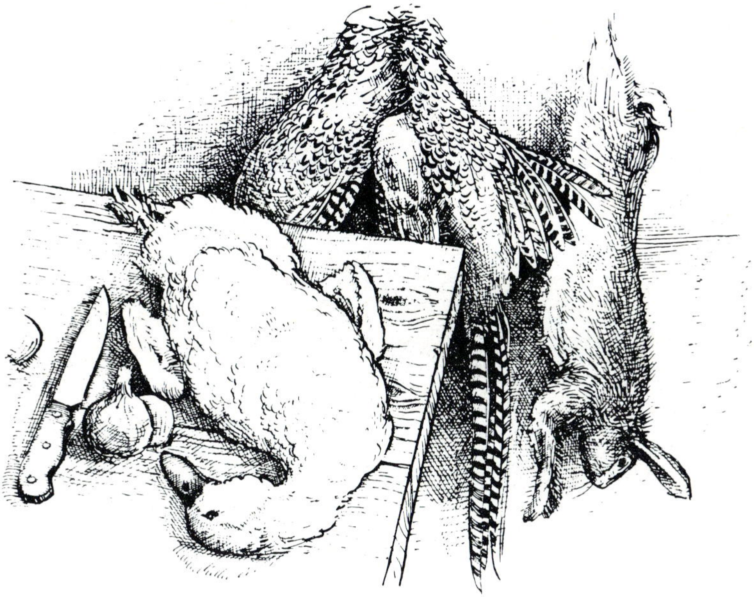

'BEFE OF ENGLAND' – A BRIEF SURVEY OF THE MEATS CONSUMED BY THE BRITISH

Amanda Goodfellow

England has always been a country of meat eaters – the Roast Beefe of Olde England is no myth. Travellers in the sixteenth, seventeenth and eighteenth centuries were amazed at the vast quantities and varieties of meat consumed. They were also impressed by its quality. Thus Fyne Moryson wrote, in the journal of his itinerary in 1617 '. . . the English Cookes, in comparison with other Nations, are most commended for roasted meates', and M. Misson, after travelling in England in the 1690s, commented: 'I always heard that they (the English) were great flesh-eaters, and I found it true . . . Among the middling sort of people they have ten or twelve sorts of common meats which infallibly take their turns at the tables, and two dishes are their dinners: a pudding, for instance, and a piece of roast beef.' Meat indeed was a staple food among those who could afford it, very little being eaten in the way of fruit and vegetables until the eighteenth century. Beef was the meat most favoured, but three- or four-year-old mutton, baby lamb, pork and sucking pig, venison and veal along with poultry and a great variety of game birds, hare and rabbit were all popular. Then as now, venison was a prerogative of the landowner, and was well regarded, particularly among the gentry in the seventeenth century (Pepys mentions many venison suppers), since the serving of it imparted a certain social *cachet*. It was always hung until high, to make it tender (unless salted), when it might be roasted and served up with a sweet spiced sauce, or made into highly seasoned pies or pasties. Hare too was popular – stuffed and roasted whole, stewed 'en civette' (1682) with white wine, vinegar, herbs and spices, jugged, or in pies shaped to the body of the animal, with the ears sticking out of the piecrust. Our ancestors liked the meat they ate to resemble the living animal. The roast meats of game birds, particularly of peacock and swan, used to be served up in their own plumage – and sucking pigs and Boars Head were made to look as life-like as possible. Jugged hare came into English printed cookery books (according to C. Anne Wilson in her excellent book *Food and Drink in Britain*) about 1720. The animal was cut up, seasoned and put into an earthenware pot or jug with no other liquid than its own blood. The jug was then put within another larger kettle of boiling water and left to simmer for three hours.

Meat was most commonly roasted on a spit and plainly served, often with an accompanying sauce made from the herbs on which the animal had fattened.

Thus laver or mint sauce was served with the highly prized lamb from salt-marsh grazing; herb-flavoured rowan jelly with mountain mutton and venison; apple sauce with apple-fed pork. New techniques of preparing meat – the 'ragoo', 'fricassee', 'braise' and 'hash' – were introduced from France in the late seventeenth century. In spite of the disapproval of the cookery experts of the time, Mrs. Glasse foremost among them, they became established favourites in the English kitchen.

The quality of meat improved considerably in the eighteenth century as a result of experiments in animal breeding and the general improvement in agricultural methods. But it was still very much fatter, and probably more highly flavoured, than the meat to which we are accustomed. Thus Per Kalm wrote after his visit of 1748: 'Roast meat is the Englishman's delice and principal dish. The English roasts are particularly remarkable for two things. All English meat . . . has a fatness and a delicious taste . . . The English men understand almost better than any other people the art of properly roasting a joint.' Fatness, indeed, was considered a virtue. Cobbett wrote in the 1820s '. . . the hog cannot be too fat . . . Lean bacon is the most wasteful thing that any family can use . . . The man who cannot live on solid fat bacon, well fed and well cured, wants the sweet sauce of labour, or is fit for the hospital.' There are men today who still prefer their bacon that way. The average lean porker raised for the modern market weighs about 120 lb. A farmer I met recently in the Lake District kills his pigs when they weigh 280 lbs. The hams alone weigh some 60 lbs. each. And the bacon, strong and salt, eaten fried in thick slices for breakfast, was all fat – only the slenderest streak of pink meat discernible in it. Bacon is traditionally associated with the farming and peasant classes. Pork meat was considered coarse fare by the upper classes. Bacon and pease pudding have been going since the Middle Ages. And in all but the hardest times, most countrymen, if they were not actually able to keep a pig or two themselves, were able to lay their hands on a little ham or pork to go with their bread, cheese and beer.

In the Middle Ages, and well into Tudor and Stuart times, meat was highly spiced – to disguise, so it is said, the fact that it was often tainted. The use of spices with savoury dishes declined as the quality of meat improved. But the difficulty of keeping meat fresh remained until the establishment of rail transport in the mid-nineteenth century and modern refrigeration methods. Until then the droving of cattle was a common feature of English life, sheep from the mountains of Wales and cattle from as far afield as Scotland being driven in herds, by easy stages, to the outskirts of London, where they were fattened before being slaughtered and sold in the London markets.

The discovery in the mid-seventeenth century that turnips could be used as winter fodder for stock meant at least that people were not condemned to a monotonous diet of salted meat throughout the winter months. But the habit of slaughtering animals in the autumn and early winter, and salting the meat, continued. It was the general practice among country farmers, as it still is among those few who still make their own bacon, to kill a pig or two at Martinmas. Anne Hughes, a farmer's wife in Herefordshire who kept a diary in 1796-7, describes how they prepared their pigs for 'thys yeres bacon' –

> 'Upp betimes thys morn, toe putt thee potts on filled wyth watter toe boyle hott for toe clene thee pigges when theye bee kylled, Carters wiffe doe com toe helpe and toe clene thee pigges innerds, a messie jobb that I doe mislyke, butte they bee verrie goode when cooked, we doe boyle them in thee bigge pott 3 dayes arter they bee well soked in bryne watter ande then John doe hav a feeste hee bein verrie swete on them, thee pigges bee hunge upp in thee oute kitchen toe coole till tomorrowe when theye wil bee cutt upp and thee mete cutt from oute them insyde, thee flytches bee then putt in thee salten ledds and rubbed wyth a mess mayde wyth 3 punds off salt, 3 punds of blacke sugger ande some salte petter and soda. Thys bee well rubbed on thee fleshie sydes wich is lefte till cum 3 dayes then wee doe turne them over puttinge more salt ande turne about for 3 weekes when we doe drayne off thee bryne, and hange itt in thee chimblie corner toe drie.'

They ate fried pig's liver and fat for supper. The next day the remaining fat was rendered into lard, and the liver, lights, hearts and tongues 'chopped up fyne wyth sweet herbes and a union' and made into faggots. Various pieces of the pig were sent off to neighbours, and finally a party was held to celebrate the end of the pigs for that year, at which was served 'pyes ande tartes, and pasties, roste pigge mete ande a grate ham and appel pudden, and a goose wyth a goodlie stuffin in hys inside toe give a flavvur, and chese freshe from thee vatte', baked potatoes, home-brewed beer and cider, cowslip and elderberry wine, and sherry – all this for eleven people. Every farmhouse had its own recipe for curing ham – some using treacle, especially in the North, some brown sugar, the sweetener counteracting the hardening action of the salt on the meat, as well as imparting flavour. The sweet-cured hams of Suffolk, pickled in beer and treacle, are still famous, and a Suffolk butcher worth his salt should be able to prepare one for you in the traditional manner. The smoking of hams is not absolutely essential, but helps to preserve them, and also adds flavour. Nowadays 'smoked' bacon is injected with pyroligneous acid, the active agent in smoke, to give it an 'authentic' flavour.

Other meats were salted, and sometimes spiced. Mutton hams were a speciality of Wales, Scotland and the border counties. And spiced salt beef was a great favourite in the eighteenth century. This is something one can no longer buy, except perhaps in London, but which one can easily make at home. I make it myself at Christmas, and have found it will keep for up to two months in a cool place. (Elizabeth David has an excellent recipe in her *Spices, Salt and Aromatics in the English Kitchen*.)

The salting, spicing and smoking of meat evolved from the need to preserve it in an edible state over a period of time. Another technique developed in the eighteenth century was that for potting meat, fish and fowl. The cooked flesh was pounded to a smooth paste with clarified butter, spices and seasoning, then packed into pots and sealed with a good layer of the same butter. England was famous for these delicacies until at least late Victorian times. Perhaps it was the amount of labour involved in their manufacture which caused potted meats to fall from favour. Nowadays it is possible to make them with very little trouble if you have a kitchen blender. They are well worth reviving.

Another dish for which the British are famous, and have remained so, is the meat pie – from the Cornish pasty and Melton Mowbray pork pies, convenient food for working men, to the splendid and elaborate Yorkshire Christmas Pyes which were still sent to friends at Christmas in the mid-nineteenth century. Hannah Glasse's recipe of 1747 instructs the cook to make a 'good standing crust' with walls and bottom very thick. This was to be filled with boned and seasoned (mace, nutmeg, cloves, pepper, salt) turkey, goose, fowl, partridge and pigeon, one inside the other, packed with diced hare on one side, and woodcock, game, wild fowl, as available, on the other. Then more seasoning was added, and four pounds of butter before the pie was closed with a thick lid and baked in a very hot oven for at least four hours. These kind of pies date from the Middle Ages, when 'coffins' of hot-water crust pastry, raised by hand, and often elaborately decorated, were filled with exotic mixtures of chopped meats, spices and candied and dried fruits. Brawn too, made from the head and foreparts of a boar or pig, has a long and honourable history. Originally something of a delicacy, eaten at feasts and Christmas time, with a mustard sauce, it is still with us, though no longer so highly regarded. The humbler black and white puddings, in all their local varieties, and the Scottish haggis, were common medieval fare. Devised as a means of using up the by-products of slaughter-time, blood, fat, marrow, entrails, they are made to traditional recipes by butchers today, especially in the North. The sausage, alas, though universally popular, has undergone a sad decline, the proportion of pork to bread crumbs and meat substitute diminishing as the price of meat has risen. Only the excellent sausages still made by the butchers of Cumberland, containing nothing but pork and seasoning, can match those appreciated by our ancestors. Here is Hannah Glasse's recipe for 'Common Sausages': 'Take 3 lbs. of nice pork, fat and lean together, without skin or grisel; chop as fine as possible, season with a teaspoonful of beaten pepper, 2 teaspoonfuls of salt, some sage shred fine, about 3 teaspoonfuls. Mix well together.' For 'Fine sausages', equal quantities of lean pork, pounded until smooth in a mortar (or chopped fine), and shredded beef suet are used, seasoned with a good deal of sage, lemon rind, sweet herbs, nutmeg, pepper and salt. When ready to use, the mixture is bound with beaten egg, shaped into cakes or sausage shapes and fried in hot butter. It could also, of course, be stuffed into skins.

The habit of eating meat is deeply ingrained in the British culture – indeed, the Victorians ascribed to it their pre-eminence among the nations of the world. But meat, particularly beef, is a very extravagant way of feeding people – twenty tons of cereal fodder being converted into only one ton of beef. If the present world-wide shortage of grain continues, it is probable that the Roast Beefe of Olde England will vanish from our tables at last.

SOURCES OF SUPPLY

Meat, game and poultry suppliers have been divided into three categories: those who can supply uncooked and smoked meats and poultry; suppliers of prepared dishes; and *pâtés*. I have also included a short-list of 'gourmet' frozen food manufacturers, who should be contacted directly for details of availability in any particular area.

PIGEON HOUSE FARM PRODUCTS LTD.

Selsey, Sussex PO20 9DT. Tel: Selsey (024 361) 4411.
Specialists in smoked poultry: smoked chicken (whole birds only); smoked capons (whole birds); smoked duckling (whole birds); smoked turkeys (whole bird, 12-16 lbs., or half bird, 6-10 lbs.); smoked turkey roll and fresh turkey roll. All supplied by mail order.

GIFTHAMS LTD.

The Quadrant, Hoylake, Wirral, Cheshire L47 2EE. Tel: (051) 632 3194.
Mild cured or lean smoked half hams, and whole hams, all supplied by mail order. Also, half or whole leg of pork, Scotch rib of beef, in minimum weights of 4 lb., 6 lb., and 10 lb. All supplied by post.

GRAYS OF WORCESTER LTD.

Orchard Street, Worcester WR5 3DP. Tel: Worcester (0905) 352388.
Whole smoked chickens, smoked capons, smoked ducks and smoked turkeys, available through mail order. Ten days notice required in all cases, orders for Christmas to reach Grays by the beginning of December. Grays can also supply unsmoked poultry: turkeys (frozen) from 10 to 20 lbs. in size; capons; ducklings; geese; pheasants (oven-ready brace, brace in feather, oven-ready cock pheasant or oven-ready hen pheasant); guinea fowl (one bird); partridge (one brace, oven-ready); wild duck (one brace, oven-ready); and venison joints (averaging three to four lbs. per joint). They can also supply joints of prime Scotch beef.

MACFISHERIES LTD.

Head Office: Ocean House, Bracknell, Berkshire RG12 2LZ. Tel: Bracknell 3111. Larger branches of Macfisheries will obtain venison to order (for personal shoppers only). Supply is erratic, however, and Macfisheries cannot guarantee availability. Worth a try if you live near one of the larger branches. For addresses, write to the head office listed above.

PAXTON AND WHITFIELD LTD.

93 Jermyn Street, London SW1Y 6JE. Tel: (01) 930 3380.
Can supply cooked and dressed York Hams, ready for table, through the post. At Christmas, in addition to this, they will also supply postal customers with uncooked York, Bradenham and Suffolk hams, and will cook them — breadcrumbed only, or baked with sugar and cloves — as required, for an additional charge. During the Christmas season, last orders to be with Paxton and Whitfield by early December.

YOUNG AND SAUNDERS LTD.

5 Queensferry Street, Edinburgh EH2 4PD. Tel: (031) 225 6075.
Can supply postal customers with Sinclairs Belfast Hams, York Hams, Bradenham (treacle cured), Epicam (sugar or treacle cured), Parma Ham, and Saxby's Pork Sausages.

CHARLES MACSWEEN

130 Bruntsfield Place, Edinburgh 10.
Will send Haggis (minimum quantity 1½ lbs.) and the less familiar Haggis Sausages, weighing 4-6 oz., useful for individual servings.

GOURMET HOSTESS FOODS LTD.

144 West Street, Marlow, Bucks. Tel: Marlow 72504.
Supply venison (haunches and saddles, rolled boned shoulder meat); partridge (farm-bred red legs, single birds, oven-ready); guinea fowl (Lancashire, roughly 1 lb. 8 oz.-1 lb. 14 oz. in size); Scottish guinea fowl (1 lb. 8 oz.-2 lb. 4 oz. in size); wood pigeon (singly or in packs of six); Cornvale quail (whole or bones) and quail livers (frozen); smoked pheasant; smoked duckling; smoked quail; smoked poussins; smoked chickens; fresh veal escalopes; calves' sweetbreads; frogs legs; Lancashire poussins; fresh calves' liver and boned chocken breasts. Smaller orders are sent first class letter post, in well insulated parcels. Larger orders are delivered locally, or sent by passenger train from the appropriate railway station, to arrive later that same evening or ready for collection the following morning.

CAVAGHAN AND GRAY LTD.

Meat Processing, Harraby, Carlisle.

ROBINSON AND SONS

Angel Lane, Penrith, Cumbria.
Both supply (to personal shoppers only) Cumberland Sausage, a pork and herb sausage traditionally associated with the region. It is sold in a continuous strip, not broken into the more familiar links.

JOHN STRANGE (BUTCHER)

High Street, Lyndhurst, Hampshire.
For venison and venison sausages, to personal shoppers only.

KING MEATS

12 King Street, Luton. Tel: Luton 25302.
Will send sausage meat (95 per cent pork, ground to a traditional Suffolk recipe) to mail order customers.

GRANTS

High Street, Croydon. Tel: (01) 688 4400.
Supply Norfolk turkeys, poultry, York and Bradenham hams and Danish gammon to postal customers (Christmas season only).

PINNEYS SMOKEHOUSES

Sternfield, Saxmundham, Suffolk.
Supply smoked Norfolk chickens (on Wednesdays only) by post.

Prepared Dishes

BUYBULK LTD.

Tunnel Bank Road, Bourne, Lincolnshire. Tel: Bourne 3291.
Bulk mail order suppliers of chicken fillets, Polish chicken and ox tongue.

DANFOOD LTD.

37 Raynham Road, Industrial Estate, Bishops Stortford, Hertfordshire.
Tel: (0279) 56399.
Will supply by post: meat balls (the Danish Middgskødboller); Danish salamis — with cognac, rum, red wine or champagne — whole or half size.

GRANTS

High Street, Croydon. Tel: (01) 688 4400.
During the Christmas season only, will supply the following to mail order customers: lambs' tongues, ox tongues, whole roast grouse, whole pheasant in wine jelly, Scottish venison in wine sauce.

YOUNG AND SAUNDERS LTD.

5 Queensferry Street, Edinburgh EH2 4PD. Tel: (031) 225 6075.
Will supply the following to mail order customers: wild duckling, guinea fowl, haggis, escargot (with or without shells). ox tongue, venison in wine sauce, whole grouse in wine sauce, quenelles nantua, roast turkey in aspic, pheasant in aspic, sweetbreads in cherry sauce, whole partridge, truffles, prepared (and smoked) frogs' legs.

GRAYS OF WORCESTER LTD.

Orchard Street, Worcester WR5 3DP. Tel: Worcester (0905) 352388.
Will supply the following to mail order customers: quails' eggs, whole stuffed chicken, crammed duck, roast goose, cornish game hen, whole grouse in port wine jelly, whole guinea fowl in red wine sauce, jugged hare, whole pheasant in burgundy sauce, whole smoked ringneck pheasant in aspic, whole pigeon in red wine sauce, whole smoked pigeon in aspic, whole quail stuffed with *pâté de foie* in sherry sauce, venison in burgundy sauce, whole wild duckling, haggis, stuffed lambs' hearts, lambs' kidneys in burgundy sauce, braised ox tail in sherry sauce, ox tongue, pigs' trotter in natural jelly, sweetbreads in sherry sauce, tripe and onions.

YE OLD PORK PIE SHOPPE

Dickinson and Morris Ltd., Melton Mowbray, Leicestershire.
Will mail the traditional Melton Mowbray raised pork pies to postal customers throughout the year. Personal shoppers also welcome.

Pâté

PIGEON HOUSE FARM PRODUCTS LTD.

Selsey, Sussex PO20 9DT. Tel: Selsey (024 361) 4411.
Will send the following pâtés by post: Chicken liver pâté de Campagne; game pâté with whisky; duck pâté with brandy; duck pâté with orange; pheasant pâté. 1 lb. minimum order in each case.

BUYBULK LTD.

Tunnel Bank Road, Bourne, Lincolnshire. Tel: Bourne 3291.
Can supply pâté de campagne, pâté de foie, pâté de foie truffé, pâté de truffé and tongue pâté in bulk by mail order. Bulk orders can also be collected from the Buybulk warehouse, through arrangement.

DANFOOD LTD.

37 Raynham Road, Industrial Estate, Bishops Stortford, Hertfordshire.
Tel: (0279) 56399.
Supply Danish liver pâté to mail order customers.

KEYLINK LTD.

Link House, Papermill Road, Sheffield S5 0EA. Tel: (07415) 2088.
Supply truffled pâté de foie gras, pure, rouleaux and crème, all imported from Perigord, by post. Minimum order: £2.30.

GRANTS

High Street, Croydon. Tel: (01) 688 4400.
Le Parfait Swiss pâté with truffles, Maitre Jacques pâté de campagne au Muscadet, Sharwoods smoked salmon pâté, terrine Louis Henry, pâté de foie gras truffé all supplied to postal customers during the Christmas season only, i.e. between October and December.

DELICATESSEN DI LORENZO LTD.

34 Old Compton Street, London W1. Tel: (01) 439 3309/3300.
Supply Belgian pâté d'Ardenne, pâté de campagne, duck and orange pâté, pheasant pâté, partridge pâté, wild boar pâté, all packed in oven-proof earthenware bowls. Mail order, at Christmas only.

PUNCHBOWL INN

Low Row, nr. Richmond, Yorkshire. Tel: Gunnerside 233.
Liver pâté and hare terrine packed in natural stone pots (½ lb. quantities) supplied mail order (Christmas season only).

YOUNG AND SAUNDERS LTD.

5 Queensferry Street, Edinburgh EH2 4PD. Tel: (031) 225 6075.
Will post the following pâtés: pâté de foie gras, pâté en terrine, purée de foie gras, mousse bloc foie d'oie truffée, pâté maison, smoked goose pâté, country

style pâté, chicken with truffle and pheasant pâté, duck with garlic pâté, smoked cod roe pâté, Isle of Arran venison or hare pâté, Cornish crab pâté, pâté foie pur porc. They can also supply pâté en croute, during the Christmas season only, for which they require ten days notice.

GRAYS OF WORCESTER LTD.

Orchard Street, Worcester WR5 3DP. Tel: Worcester (0903) 352388.
Will supply the following pâtés by mail order throughout the year: country style pâté, chicken liver truffle pâté, duck liver pâté with garlic, chicken liver and pheasant pâté, pâté de canard à l'orange, a range of American pâtés (smoked turkey, pheasant, smoked rainbow trout), game pâté, pâté de foie, patum peperium and smoked cod roe pâté. Can also supply by post the following terrines: de marcassin (young wild boar pâté), de lièvre, du canard.

THORESBY CATERERS

North Thoresby, Grimsby DN36 5RL.
Can supply game paté to mail order customers.

Frozen Foods (Meat and Poultry)

Criticisms of frozen food are all too often justified, but they can be a great deal better than their name suggests, and — assuming you already own a freezer — their usefulness cannot be disputed. Only a very few of the frozen food manufacturers specialise in the 'gourmet' end of the market, however, and their products do have to be searched for, as they do not generally benefit from the sort of massive distribution enjoyed by the more 'popular' frozen food ranges.

The following producers all specialise in high quality frozen dishes, and retail through most of the better food halls and some delicatessens. Should you have any difficulty in tracking down your nearest stockist, by all means write to the company concerned for further information, as they will be pleased to help.

ALVESTON KITCHENS LTD.

Timothy's Bridge Road, Stratford-upon-Avon, Warwickshire CV37 9NH.
One of the biggest of the 'specialist' frozen food producers, their range includes Pâté de Campagne, Duckling à l'Orange, Duckling with Honey and Chestnuts, Coq au Vin, Chicken Basquaise, Boeuf Bourguignon, Fillet of Pork, Escalope of Veal (highly praised in a recent *Good Housekeeping* survey), Celery and Ham, Chicken Mornay, and an enormously wide range of cheesecakes and American desserts from the Sara Lee range (distributed in the UK only by Alveston Kitchens). Alveston distribute their foods nationally, mainly through depart-

ment store food halls and the better delicatessens, but in case of difficulty, write direct to the company for further information.

CROFT FARM FOODS

Chadwick End Village, West Midlands B93 9BP. Tel: Lapworth 2161.
A wide range of poultry dishes and pâtés, including Chicken Marengo, Coq au Vin, Duckling with Orange, Farmhouse Pâté, Halibut Normandy, Haddock Portuguese, Fish Italiano, Chicken Royal, Boeuf Bourguignon and Stroganoff, Cottage Terrine and Moussaka. Again, in case of difficulty, write directly to the producer for further information.

JUGG FOODS LTD.

Their standard range includes Moussaka, Chicken with Peppers, Jugged Lamb, Hunter's Chicken, Poussin with Grapes, Burgundy Beef, Duckling with Oranges and Fisherman's Pie. Distributed nationally through larger branches of the Waitrose chain, department store food halls and some delicatessens.

Smoked Fish

SMOKED FISH

An Introduction by G. R. Watkin

The present near perfection of our smoked fish is a result not only of the refining of curing techniques but reflects many social changes. Smoke as a preservative of food was in natural sequence to the use of fire to cook – smoke dried out the moisture, covered the food with antiseptic substances and (incidentally) kept the flies away. The use of salt is of nearly as great an antiquity and marked the transition from hunter to farmer. Cereals do not supply the salts of natural meat, so that primitively prepared salt was physically required as well as being useful as a preservative.

The need for preservation then was to even out supplies, to hold food from the glut periods for use in the lean days – lean days not only of fish supply, but of protein in general. Before the introduction of winter feed crops for food animals in the eighteenth century, the eating of salt fish during Lent was a matter not of piety but of necessity. It was all the protein left before the new season's meat became available after Easter.

In the nineteenth century, the industrial revolution had its effect on preserved fish. The steam trawler and drifters landed fish in industrial quantities, the railways distributed the fish quickly and efficiently, the first mechanically produced ice kept the fish in better condition. Perhaps even more important was the shift of population from agrarian to industrial employment, which put cash and therefore buying power into the hands of many who had previously raised their own food. This was the point at which the preserving of fish ceased to be a cottage industry born of necessity and became part of a food industry that had to sell its product. So consumer choice and technological innovation went hand in hand to modify and improve the quality of preserved fish. Not before time if we consider the advice of a Dr. S. Nelson, who in 1753 warned parents that, 'Fish is a sort of diet extremely improper for children', while another writer complained that curing left fish 'in a condition that demands the greatest efforts by the stomach to extract the food value from the fibrous masses'.

The role of the curer now began to change as both cooling and rapid transport rendered less necessary the efforts to prevent spoilage. The curer could now concentrate on flavour, and no longer needed to extract so much moisture from the fish that it became dry and fibrous. He no longer had to add so much salt that the fish had to be soaked for days before cooking so that its texture was broken and flabby. So were born the relatively lightly smoked cured products we now know.

Every smoke curing process involves four stages. Firstly the fish must be prepared and each product has its own needs and each production centre its own quirks. Whether a Finnan Haddock has its backbone left or right of the central cut indicates to the initiate whether it was cured in Aberdeen or London.

Secondly, a salting stage, either by brine or dry salting. Brine is quicker and rarely are fish exposed to it for more than twenty minutes while dry salting may take hours or even days.

Both salting processes leave the fish wet and wet fish do not smoke well, as they fail to form that glossy pellicle which decorates the cut surface of well-cured fish. Therefore the third stage is one of dripping to ensure at least surface dryness.

At last, the smoking itself. The temperature of the smoking kiln decides the nature of the finished product. Cold smoking, where the temperature remains below 85°F, is used for products such as kippers which are normally cooked before consumption; whereas hot smoked products, having been subjected to kiln temperatures of perhaps 200°F, are ready to eat.

Traditional smoking kilns betray in their form their origin as domestic chimneys. Modified and purpose built, they nevertheless show the rectilinear structure and draught-producing height, capped by a cowl that once topped the wood-burning hearth of the old-time farmhouse kitchen. Such kilns, in the hands of a master smoker, produce a delicious variety of smoked fish, but therein lies the rub — variation is not always the aim of the curer. The variety is produced by the vagaries of our climate: the speed of the wind, the humidity of the atmosphere, the temperature of the night air. These uncontrollable factors mean that the traditional kiln is of no use to the industrial producer as the products are not uniform, the results not plannable, the yield not predictable. For the factory operation, the mechanical kiln with its controlled temperature, drying rate and smoke density produces smoked fish of perhaps monotonous uniformity, tailored, as so many food products are these days, not so much to please but rather not to offend.

Therefore in choosing our supplier of smoked fish we have a choice between the steady, level, unexceptionable quality of the factory product or the highs and lows of the traditional smoker. Let us not delude ourselves about the lows. They do occur and perhaps our best guard against them, as in so many food choices, is the finding and nurturing of a good retailer. A retailer who is a craftsman, immersed in the language and lore of his class. In nurturing him, pander to his vanity by asking his advice and then follow it. Be thoughtful of his difficulties and sensible in your demands. Try not to blame him if you plan a menu which includes bloater pâté in August or buckling complete with roes in April, and he politely regrets that he cannot help. Bloaters, cured with their guts intact, can only be made in the cooler months and April is one of the few months when herrings from somewhere round our coasts are not filled with roe.

It is not as if your choice of smoked fish is limited. We are particularly blessed in these islands with the variety, quality and flavour of our fish, caught in cold northern waters. It seems to be universally acknowledged that with few exceptions, the cold water fish have superior flavour. So starting with good fish, and with techniques refined over the years, it is small wonder that we can produce so many varieties of delicious smoked fish, that it becomes difficult to decide where to start in their introduction.

Chats, Kits, Gibbers and Jumbos – how's that for an introduction? Chats are too small and Jumbos too big – for making Finnans at least; these are trade names for sizes of haddocks and it is the middle two that provide the material for this delectable product. Finnans are split, until almost flat (but never filleted), brined and cold smoked, but how much brine and how much smoke is the question and the answer usually comes out – 'distribution'. If the fish is to be eaten within a day or two of curing then the producer can afford the luxury of the London Cure or the subtleties of the Glaswegian Pale Cure. If distribution is to be longer, then a harder cure will be required.

It is generally agreed that much of the flavour of animal foods is lost when they are separated from their bones and cooked, and one therefore hesitates to mention smoked fillets and golden cutlets. The former can be made from any white fish including haddock, the latter from small haddocks and whitings only. I believe that when they are well produced, and there are many that are not, they have a place in the preparation of dishes where smoked fish is an ingredient and where the convenience of the cook compensates for the undoubted loss of flavour which may be mitigated by the interaction of other ingredients. Fish pies and kedgeree are suitable dishes for the use of fillets.

Hot smoking converts a pair of haddocks, their tails tied together, into Arbroath smokies. With their crisp brown skins and juicy interiors they can be eaten cold, but try them covered by bacon rashers, placed under a slow grill so that as they warm the bacon fat combines with them to remedy their only deficiency.

The herring with its higher integral fat content lends itself to many varieties of cure. Kippering, a term originally applied to a method of curing salmon, is the process most frequently used. Invented by John Woodger of Seahouses in the 1840s, its processing changed little until the Second World War when an order from the Food Minister, indirectly and doubtlessly unforeseen, gave rise to a very basic change. The order required that all food should be sold by weight, not by number, and this practice persists to the present day. All curing removes moisture and therefore weight. While sale was by number this did not matter. Once sale was by weight, there was an incentive to cure as little as possible. To maintain the appearance of the undercured kipper, many curers resorted to the use of dye. While it would be unrealistic to condemn the use of all dyes in foodstuffs, their purpose should be honestly acknowledged. Undyed kippers are available, cured on the Isle of Man and sold generally in North-West England, but they are not to everybody's taste.

The producers of bloaters are in need of encouragement, as they believe that the demand for their product, with its dry crackly skins and robust flavour, is diminishing. In a morass of blandness, the distinctive flavour of bloaters is a high point to be cherished.

Changing and more catholic tastes have increased the demand for and therefore the production of, more hot smoked fish. The buckling prepared from herrings, crinkled, golden, rich, ready to be eaten or made into a pâté; smoked mackerel, food for gourmand as well as gourmet; smoked rainbow trout, too delicate in flavour for the often suggested horseradish sauce; rich succulent smoked eel, caught on the eve of its departure from fresh water bound for its spawning grounds in the distant Sargasso.

And now from crescendo to climax, to the ultimate perfection of flavour, to the orange-red glory of smoked Scottish salmon. Sides cut from the most beautiful of all fish (an aside: beauty is in the eye of the human observer. When near to spawning and in need of attracting a mate, their beauty is considerably diminished — that is, to a human observer), laid in dry salt, for perhaps a day, allowed to dry and then gently cold-smoked with that touch of juniper in the smoke. Never cooked, never in need of cooking, the translucent slices require no accompaniments and yet consider adding to perfection by stuffing rolls of smoked salmon with white crab meat, bound with a little cream flavoured with pepper and lemon juice.

May I, in conclusion, leave a thought, almost an admonition, with you. Those of us who are aware of good food and who actively seek it out should not become too precious. We should not become too scathing about the deficiencies of factory-produced food. We should recognise that we live in an urban society where the need to provide huge quantities of comestibles is daily met by our food industry. However blandly, however uniformly they carry out this task, they do at least ensure that everyone in the country has a chance to obtain a nutritious diet.

We must continue not only to achieve high standards of our own choice, but in doing so encourage by example the adoption of higher standards by all and being 'ever mindful of the needs of others', we must remember that the food we seek is not only at the top of a pyramid of taste but also an economic pyramid. Without an infra-structure of fish fingers only the sheikhs would eat smoked salmon.

SOURCES OF SUPPLY

DARTSIDE SMOKED FISHERIES LTD.

The Old Racecourse, Totnes. Tel: Totnes 863525/863350.
Can supply the following to mail order customers: local Dart smoked salmon, boned and rolled; smoked salmon sides (sliced or unsliced); smoked salmon pâté (2 oz., 6 oz., and 1 lb. quantities); smoked rainbow trout (whole or sliced, the latter in ½ lb. packs); smoked mackerel (whole, fillets and pâté); smoked sprats; smoked haddock (skinned fillets, finnan fillets); smoked King Silver eels, supplied whole; smoked cods' roe, in 6 oz. and 1 lb. quantities; queen scallops.

PIGEON HOUSE FARM PRODUCTS LTD.

Selsey, Sussex PO20 9DT. Tel: Selsey (024 361) 4411.
Smoked Canadian Salmon (sliced, minimum order ½ lb., whole side only, 2¾-3¼ lbs.); smoked Scotch salmon (sliced, minimum order, ½ lb., whole side only, up to 2½ lbs.); smoked trout (1 lb. minimum order); smoked mackerel (1 lb. minimum order). All available by post.

AFOODS GROUP LTD.

Ambassador House, Brigstock Road, Thornton Heath, Surrey. Tel: 01 689 1861.
Supplies available only during the cooler winter months, from October to March inclusive. Smoked Scotch salmon, sides (2 lb. and 2½ lb. approx.), sliced (2½ lb. packs), finely sliced (1 lb. boxes); smoked rainbow trout, in packs of four fish (minimum weight, 1½ lbs.).

GEO. DEVEREAU AND SONS LTD.

38 Strand Street, Douglas, Isle of Man. Tel: Douglas 3257/3258/6360.
Kippers by post, in parcels containing 2, 3, 4, 5 or 6 pairs of fish.

GIFTHAMS LTD.

The Quadrant, Hoylake, Wirral, Cheshire L47 2EE. Tel: 051 632 3194.
Smoked Irish salmon, in 2 lb. and 2½ lb. sizes, supplied to postal customers.

LOCHINVAR

Marine Harvest, Greyhope Road, Aberdeen AB9 2JA.
Mail order suppliers of smoked (Scottish) salmon: whole sides (from 1½ lbs.-5½ lbs.) sliced, interleaved smoked salmon and smoked salmon pâté (minimum order 1 lb.).

BISHOPS AND JACKSON LTD.

37 Woodland Way, Woodford Wells, Essex.
Smoked Scottish salmon in 2 and 3 lb. sides, 1 lb. boxes of sliced smoked salmon, supplied to postal customers during the winter months.

NEEDHAMS

Pontypool, Monmouthshire NP4 6JW. Tel: 04955 55698.
Sides of smoked salmon (Scottish) in 1½ lb. to 3 lb. sides. Also 1 lb. packs of sliced smoked salmon.

THE SMOKEHOUSE

P. O. Box 19, 44a Cleethorpe Road, Grimsby, South Humberside DN31 3LE.
Smoked salmon in 5 lb. boxes, mailed to postal customers during the winter months.

RITCHIE BROS.

37 Watergate, Rothesay 11, Scotland.
Scottish smoked salmon in 8 oz., 1 lb., 1½ lb. and 2 lb. packs, sliced smoked salmon sides in 2 lb. packs, kippers. Mailed to postal customers.

J. M. SHEARER

8 Victoria Street, Aberdeen AB9 1FL. Tel: 0224 28206.
Smoked salmon (2 lb., 2½ lb., 3 lb. sides), sliced smoked salmon (1 lb. boxes); pack of four smoked rainbow trout; 2 lb. packs of smoked whole eel. Postal customers only.

L. ROBSON AND SONS

Craster, Alnwick, Northumberland.
Craster kippers (herrings smoked over oak-chip fires) available in varying quantities to postal customers.

T. MOORE AND SONS

Mill Road, Peel, Isle of Man.
Kippers (in packs of various quantities) sent to postal customers.

HENRY SUTTON

Great Yarmouth.
Red and black herrings, kippers. Write to Suttons for details of availability, as it

varies.

R. AND R. SPINK

6 Brothock Bridge, Arbroath, Angus. Tel: Arbroath 3246.
Arbroath Smokies (haddock gutted and decapitated, but not split – as Finnan haddock are – and unsmoked, ready to eat) supplied in packs of two pairs to postal customers.

YOUNG AND SAUNDERS LTD.

5 Queensferry Street, Edinburgh EH2 4PD. Tel: 031 225 6075.
Smoked salmon (in sides or sliced); smoked trout; smoked cods' roe; smoked sturgeon. All supplied to postal customers. Also available (prepared, pre-packed or otherwise): clams, Pacific Coast oysters, smoked oysters, Danish mussels, skewered octopus, minced clams, Gulf Belle oysters, Rainbow Trout fillets, smoked eel fillets and smoked octopus.

GRAYS OF WORCESTER LTD.

Orchard Street, Worcester WR5 3DP. Tel: Worcester (0905) 352388.
Smoked (Scottish) salmon in 2 lb. and 3½ lb. sides, sliced in ½ lb. and 1 lb. packs; smoked trout (supplied in packs of six fish, weighing approx. 2 lbs. in all); smoked eel (1 lb. packs); smoked cods' roe (1 lb. packs). Pre-packaged or prepared fish: smoked Colorado trout; baby clams; mussels in natural juice, Fiskebøller, boiled oysters, Rainbow Trout à la Meunière, sliced smoked salmon (frozen).

DANFOOD LTD.

37 Raynham Road, Industrial Estate, Bishops Stortford, Herfordshire.
Tel: 0279 56399.
Herrings (marinated fillets, roll mops), mussels (fried in butter, smoked in oil, in brine, in cream sauce, mussel soup), tinned shrimps, Fiskebøller, herrings in red wine. All available by post only.

GOURMET HOSTESS FOODS

144 West Street, Marlow, Bucks. Tel: Marlow 72504.
Smoked salmon (whole sides, or sliced in ½ lb. quantities); smoked English lake trout; smoked cods' roe in 1-2 lb. packs; smoked eel fillets; smoked mackerel (headless, in cases containing 30 fish, each weighing 5 to 6 oz.); scallops; local Flookborough potted shrimps in butter; locally caught whitebait; Scottish crabmeat (white) from the claw only; brown or white crabmeat; langoustes (rock

lobster); Long Island oysters (on the half shell, separately packed in boxes of four); jumbo scampi, shell and tail on, head off; Quenelles de Brochet, imported fresh or frozen from France; Icelandic, Malasian and Mediterranean prawns; local Fleetwood and homewater scampi (spring and summer only) in two grades. All available to postal customers.

PINNEYS SMOKEHOUSES

Sternfield, Saxmundham, Suffolk.
Supply smoked salmon, eel (fillets) and trout in packs of varying sizes to postal customers.

BAXTERS

Poulton Square, Morecombe.
Potted Morecombe Bay shrimps – the genuine article – supplied in quantities of 200 grms. to postal customers.

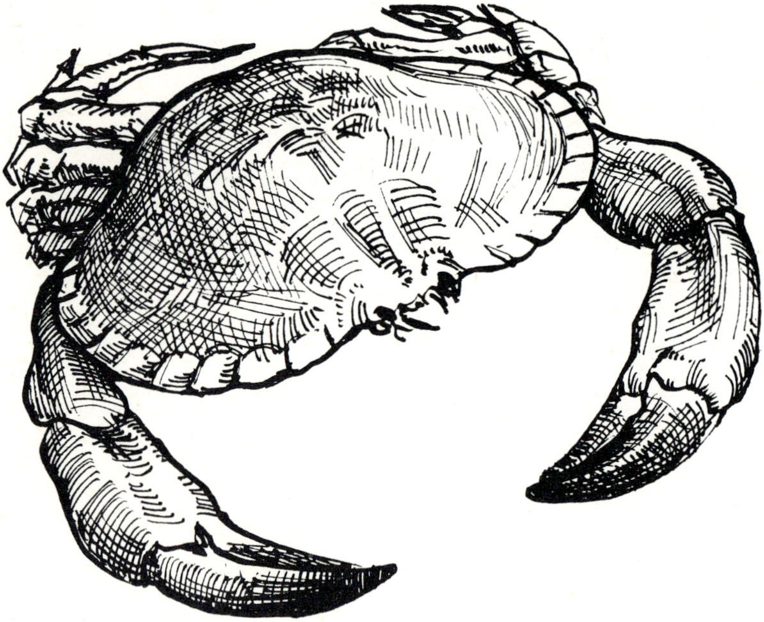

Fruit and Vegetables, Herbs and Spices

FRUIT AND VEGETABLES

It is a sad but simple truth that we take our fruits and vegetables for granted. Choice is enormous, seasonal constraints no longer limit availability, and there are quite literally thousands of shops and stores where it is possible to buy fruit and vegetables and be reasonably content with what appears to be good value for money.

But it is equally true that people are beginning to look with something akin to suspicion at the produce piled so lavishly (and wrapped so tightly) on supermarket shelves – and learning to complain when less than scrupulous greengrocers 'serve from the back', concealing bruised, over-ripe fruit or frost-bitten vegetables from the customer's eye. We are starting to learn that availability is no guarantee of freshness, that choice does not necessarily imply quality.

Which is why, in this section, I have chosen to concentrate, first of all, on markets. Markets are enjoyable places to shop in, for a start, but there are perfectly sound reasons for braving the bustle and chaos of a market place, treating it not just as a source of local colour but as a sensible place to shop. It is worth remembering that a stall-holder cannot rely on passing trade for his regular custom. He opens for only two or three days in any week, and often mans his stall only once in seven days. He cannot hope to compete with a high street greengrocer operating a regular five-day week, unless he can be sure of offering consistently higher quality at the same or slightly lower prices. In many cases, the market stall-holder buys his produce from one or two local farms, or he may grow it in his own market garden. Look for long queues – they may be tiresome but they invariably attest to the quality of the produce available from the stall concerned. And if there is a Women's Institute market stall in your local market, then by all means sample their produce. Some of the WI stalls may sell only preserves and cakes, but when members have fruit and vegetables for sale they are nearly always of the highest quality and represent very good value. In a market survey recently conducted by the *Observer*, the WI stalls were consistently singled out for favourable comment, and it would seem that their stalls (and their own, independent markets) really are worth searching for. They operate under the same series of trading and hygiene regulations as any other stall-holder, and, if anything, observe the letter and the spirit of the law more scrupulously. The listings that follow include details of WI market stalls operating within other markets, together with information on WI markets operating quite separately.

Of the shops and stores I have singled out for comment, I have had to be ruthlessly selective. On the whole, the shops mentioned either grow their own food, or buy from local farms which have established a reputation for extremely high quality. In some cases, the shops are what might be described as health food shops, which could provoke the lift of an eyebrow or two. I tend to feel that health food shops are usually more of a hindrance than a help. Their prices are invariably high, they are often crammed with the more nonsensical and lunatic of health food preparations (so-called) and there is more than a hint of cranki-ness about many of them. But there are a good many exceptions to the rule, and I hope that the comparatively few in number that have been included are worthy representatives of all that is most acceptable about health food – and all that is exceptional. For again, it is worth remembering that when a concern for the quality and freshness of food is an honest one, it corresponds very closely to the gourmet's interest in searching out the best available, in order to enjoy food at its best. In this one respect, the gourmet shares a common interest with the 'wholefooder', or the health food freak – and as good food gets more and more difficult to find, it might be worth forgetting the differences and celebrating those areas of mutual agreement by at least visiting the shops in question and try-ing out for yourself some of the produce available. It doesn't necessarily mean foregoing the pleasures of the more exotic fruits and vegetables either. Even the health food fringe has adapted well to changes in popular taste, and reflects these changes in an increasingly wide variety of produce available.

SOURCES OF SUPPLY

The following list of markets and shops has been arranged by county, listed alphabetically:

BEDFORDSHIRE

Bedford
Bedford Market, St. Pauls Square (Wed., Sat.).
Fruit and vegetables especially good (visit A. G. Alex's stall, or Iliads of Wis-bech). WI market stall Wed. 8.30-12.30.

Ampthill
Ampthill Market, Market Square.
WI market stall, Thurs. 8.30-12.00.

Dunstable
Dunstable Market.
WI market stall, Market Place, Wed. 9.00-12.00.

Leighton Buzzard
General market, Wed., Sat. Particularly good for fruit, vegetables (Spalding Nurseries) and fish.

BERKSHIRE

Abingdon
WI market, Fridays, 9.30-12.00, St. Nicholas Church Hall.

Cookham
WI market. The Pindar Hall, Cookham Rise, Fridays 9.00-12.00.

Newbury
Market Square, Thurs., Sat. WI market stall Thurs. 8.00-1.00.
Most greengrocery stalls in the market good for fruit and vegetables. Look out also for fish, locally produced free-range eggs.

Reading Market
WI market, Tues., Fri. 8.30-3.30, 2 London Street.

Tilehurst
WI market, Thurs. 8.30-11.00, Polstead Road.

Twyford
WI market, The Court Room, Alms Houses, Thurs. 9.30-11.30.

Wokingham
WI market, The Methodist Centre, Rose Street, Fri. 9.30-11.30.

BRECONSHIRE

Brecon
Seasonal WI market, Market Hall, Fridays 9.00-1.30.

Haye on Wye
WI market, White House Cafe, Sat. 10.00-1.00.

BUCKINGHAMSHIRE

Aylesbury
WI market stall, The Friars Square, Sat. 8.00-12.00.

Bletchley
Market currently in temporary position, due to be moved. Thurs., Sat. Good for fruit and vegetables.

Buckingham
WI stall, Market Place, Sat. 8.30-12.00.

Chesham
Nashleigh Hill Nurseries, Ltd., 20 Red Lion Street.
Fresh fruit from The Lee, fresh vegetables from Chestnut Tree Farm, Beds. Also worth looking at their dairy produce, free-range eggs and bread.

High Wycombe
WI market, Bat and Ball, The Common, Fri. 8.30-12.30.

Princes Risborough
'Bonkers' Garden Centre, Church Street.
Fresh fruit, herbs and vegetables in season from local producers.

Thame
Seasonal WI market, Town Centre, Tues. 8.30-12.00.

CAMBRIDGESHIRE

Cambridge
Market Hill. Daily.
Fruit (apples especially) and vegetables. Also worth shopping in the market for shellfish, cheese. WI market stall Thurs, 8.00-12.00.

Ely
Market Place, Thursdays.
Fruit and vegetables good. Also fish, particularly shellfish, and dairy produce (cheese, pork pies, butter, farm-produced pork sausages).

CARMARTHENSHIRE

Carmarthen
Market Place, Wed., Sat.
Fruit and vegetables good. WI stall Sat. 8.00-1.00. Look out also for regional specialities — laverbread, cockles, Welsh salt bacon — all available in the market. Eggs, meat and freshly baked bread all available.

Llandello
Market Place, WI stall, Sat. 8.30-1.00.

Llanelli
Covered Market (adjoining new shopping precinct), Thurs., Sat.
Fruit and vegetables, extremely fresh and a wide variety available. Look at the meat stalls, too.

Amanford
Primrose Stores, 30 Quay Street.
Sells organically grown vegetables and fresh herbs.

CHESHIRE

Chester
Market Hall, daily.
Fruit and vegetables, meat (Parkinson and Son particularly good), dairy produce (naturally including the various Cheshire cheeses, including Cheshire Blue), bacon and poultry. WI market stall Friday, 9.30-1.00.

Crewe
Monday morning. Fri., Sat.
Fresh fruit and vegetables and worth shopping there for cheese and meat.

Knutsford
Market Hall, Silkmill Street, WI stall Sat. 9.00-12.30.

Macclesfield
Indoor market (Grosvenor Centre Precinct), outdoor market (Town Centre). Indoor operates Tuesday-Saturday, outdoor market open Tuesday, Friday and Saturday. Vegetables and fruit, cheese worth shopping for.

Nantwich
Market Square, WI market stall, Thurs. 10.00-1.00.

Neston
WI market, Neston Town Hall, Fri. 8.30-3.00.

Sandbach
The Commons, Thurs., Sat.
Fruit and vegetables (nearly all locally produced) and cheese worth shopping for.

Stockport
Outdoor market, Fri., Sat.
Fruit and vegetables. At the same time, visit the Hen Market, for dairy produce in general and cheese in particular.

Wilmslow
Friday only. Fruit and vegetables, and cheese from The Jersey Man stall.

CORNWALL

Bude
Wonnacotts Dairy, 4 Lansdown Road.
Fruit and vegetables from the dairy's own farm.

Callington
WI market, WI Hall, Weds. 10.00-12.00.

Falmouth
WI market, St. Mary's RC Church Hall, Fri. 9.15-12.15.

Cambourne
WI market, St. Martins Church Hall, Fri. 2.00-4.00.

Helston
WI market stall, Corn Exchange, Fri. 9.00-12.00.

Launceston
Adjacent to the cattle market, Tues., Sat.
Fruit, vegetables and dairy produce good.

Liskeard
WI market, Isaac Foot Memorial Hall, Fri. 9.00-11.30.

Penzance
General market, Tues., Thurs., Sat. WI market, St. Johns Hall, Thurs. 9.15-12.00.

Redruth
Thomas, The Square, Portreath. Organically grown vegetables.

Porscatho
WI market, Memorial Hall, seasonal, Fri. 2.15-3.45.

St. Austell
General market daily. WI market, Congregational Schoolroom, Fri. 8.30-11.45.

Tintagel
Seasonal WI market, WI Hall, Wed. 10.00-12.00.

Truro
WI market, 68 Lemon Street, Wed. 8.55-12.30.

S. Piper and Sons, 1 Francis Street.
Fresh, locally grown fruit and vegetables.

Veryan
WI market, British Legion Hall, Fri. 2.30-3.30 (Oct.-June); 10.30-11.30 (June-Sept.).

CUMBERLAND

Brampton
WI market, Moot Hall, 9.30-11.30, Wed.

Carlisle
Market Place, Monday-Sat.
Fruit and vegetables, meat. WI stall Wed., Fri. 8.30-12.00 in the Fish Market.

Cockermouth
Seasonal WI market, Mitchells Estate Rooms. Fri. 10.00-12.00.

Keswick
Moot Hall, Sats.
Fruit and vegetables particularly recommended. Shop for meat and poultry at the same time.

Penrith
WI market, Market Hall, Devonshire Street. Tues. 8.30-12.15.

Whitehaven
WI market, YWCA Lowther Street, Thurs. 11.00-1.00.

Wigton
Market Hall, WI market stall, Tues. 9.00-1.30.

CO. DURHAM

Consett
Market Square, Friday, Saturday.
Fruit and vegetables and dairy produce.

South Shields
James Quigley, 291-297 Prince Edward Road.
Enormous range of fresh fruits.

DENBIGHSHIRE

Denbigh
WI market, County Hall, High Street, Fri. 9.00-11.30.

DEVON

Barnstaple
WI stall in the Pannier Market, Fri. 8.00-1.00.
Fruit, vegetables and dairy produce available (and good) in the general market, weekdays.

Bideford
Pannier Market, Tues., Sat. WI market stall, 13-14 Butchers Row, Sat. 6.30-12.00.

Bow
WI market, Main Street, Sat. 9.00-1.00.

Culm Valley (Tiverton)

WI market produce stall in Tiverton Market, Market Hall, Fri. 8.30-12.00.

Dartmouth

WI market produce stall in Dartmouth Butter Market Hall, Fri. 9.00-12.30.

Exbourne

Seasonal WI market, forecourt of the Red Lion Inn, Fri. 3.00-4.30.

Exeter

St. Georges Market, Fore Street, Mon-Sat. WI market stall, Thurs, 8.00-2.30, Sat. 8.00-2.30.

Fruit and vegetables excellent quality. Devon cream usually obtainable.

Holsworthy

Market Place, Wednesdays.

Kingsbridge

WI market stall, Kingsbridge Town Hall, Thurs. 9.30-12.30.

Newton Abbot

Market Hall, Wed. and Sat. WI market stall, Wed. 8.30-1.00,

Okehampton

Market Hall, Sat.

Fruit and vegetables, dairy produce and fish.

Plymouth

The Market, Mon.-Sat. WI market stall, Tues. 8.30-1.30.

Fruit and vegetables, dairy produce, cold meats (V. Grylls), fish.

Sidmouth

Market Hall. WI market stall, Fri. 8.00-12.30.

Tavistock

Pannier Market, Friday; WI market stall, Fri. 8.00-12.30.

Fruit and vegetables, fresh chicken, cakes and pies.

DORSET

Blandford

The Shambles, Market Place. WI market stall, Thurs. 8.00-1.00.

Bridport

WI market, WI Hall, West Street, Sat. 8.00-12.30.

Dorchester

WI market, Congregational School Room, Charles Street, Fri. 8.30-11.45.

Gillingham
WI market, Methodist Church Hall, Fri. 9.30-12.00.

Lowmans Stores, 2 Wyke Street. Locally grown fruit and vegetables available in season.

Sherborne
Seasonal WI market, Methodist School, Cheap Street, Thurs. 9.00-12.00.

Sturminster Newton
Corn Exchange, Cattle Market. WI market stall, Mon. 10.30-1.30.

Wareham
General Market, Thurs. WI market, Methodist Church Hall, North Street, Thurs. 8.30-3.00.

Wimborne
General Market, Tues. (poultry, fruit and vegetables), Friday. WI market, Fri. 9.30-12.00, Church House.

Wyke Regis
WI market, WI Hall, Gallway Road, Fri. 9.00-1.30.

DUNBARTONSHIRE

Helensburgh
A. Bulloch and Co., 32 West Clyde Street, Dunbartonshire.
Locally grown fruit and vegetables, as well as many other delicacies, including trout and salmon.

ESSEX

Basildon
Shopping Precinct, Tues., Fri., Sat.
Fruit and vegetables, fish and aggs all good.

Braintree
Town Centre, Wed.
Farm produce, including consistently good fruit and vegetables. Also excellent fish market, on the same day.

WI market, 14 New Street, Wed., Fri. 9.00-4.00.

Chelmsford
Shopping Precinct, Town Centre, Tues., Fri., Sat.
Fruit and vegetables (Mackenzie's stall singled out as particularly good). WI stall.

Colchester
WI market, Tues.-Sat. 8.30-3.45, 13 Pelhams Lane.

H. Gunton, 81/83 Crouch Street, Colchester. Specialist greengrocers and delicatessen.

Epping
Seasonal WI market, High Street, Mon. 8.00-2.00.

Halstead
WI market, Club Room, 'Royal Oak', Fri. 9.30-12.30.

Harlow
WI market shop, weekdays (early closing, 2.00 on Wed.), 9.00-4.30, Post Office Walk.

Peldon
Peldon Village Hall, WI market, Sat. 11.00-12.30.

Romford
Romford Shopping Precinct, Wed., Fri., Sat.
Especially good for fruit and vegetables, fish and free-range eggs.

Saffron Walden
WI market, Fri. 8.30-2.30, 11 George Street.

Southend
Southend United FC car park, Tues., Thurs.
Fruit and vegetables and meat particularly worth buying here.

Walton-on-the-Maze
Old Walton Vicarage Site (Town Centre), Thursday.
Fruit and vegetables and free-range eggs.

West Mersea
WI market, WI Hall, third Saturday in every month, 10.00-12.00.

Wickford
Near Wickford Railway Station, Monday.
Fruit and vegetables, and particularly notable for fish.

Yeldham
Seasonal WI market, Reading Room forecourt, High Street, Fri. 2.30-4.30.

GLAMORGAN

Cardiff

Weekdays. Fruit and vegetables, farm produce in general, meat and poultry (Morgans stall), fish (Ashton's), bacon and ham.

Quadrille Health Store, 77 Pontcanna Street, Cathedral Road.

A health food store that also stocks fresh fruit and vegetables from a local nursery when in season.

Cowbridge
WI market, Lesser Hall, High Street, Fri. 10.30-12.00.

Neath
Mon-Sat. Fruit and vegetables and meat worth buying.

Oystermouth
Seasonal WI market, Town Hall, Fri. 10.30-12.00.

Port Talbot
Port Talbot Health Foods, Market Hall.
Another health food store, but worth visiting to sample their Boxford Farm apples (not always available), avocado pears, amd other fruits.

Swansea
Wed., Sat. Fruit and vegetables, laverbread (for the brave), free-range eggs, Welsh butter and cheeses, and fish — including locally caught cockles and mussels.

GLOUCESTERSHIRE

Badgeworth
WI market, 'Simali', Fri. 3.30-5.00.

Bourton-on-the-Water
WI market, Church Room, Fri. 10.00-12.00.

The Old Bakehouse, 3 Sherborne Street.
Fresh, locally grown vegetables and fresh herbs from their own gardens.

Cirencester
Market Place, Wed., Thurs., Fri., Sat. WI market stall also on those days, between 8.00 and 5.00.

Moreton-in-the-Marsh
WI market, WI Hall, New Street, Thurs. 10.00-11.30.

Nailsworth
Town Hall, WI market stall, Fri. 9.00-10.45.

Painswick
Town Hall, WI market stall, Fri. 10.30-11.30.

Stroud
The Shambles, WI market stall, Fri. 9.30-2.00.

Tetbury

WI market, Town Hall, Fri. 9.30-12.00.

Tewkesbury
General market, Wed., Sat.

WI market, The Ancient Grudge, High Street, Fri. 9.45-11.45.

Thornbury
WI market, Church Institute, St. Mary Street, Wed. 10.00-12.00.

Wotton-under-Edge
Town Hall, WI market stall, Fri. 9.30-12.15.

HAMPSHIRE

Alton
Open air market, town centre. Tuesday.
Fruit and vegetables particularly good and fresh. Also, a WI market stall, Assembly Rooms, Fri. 9.15-12.00.

Andover
WI market stall, The Guildhall, Fri. 9.00-12.00.

Basingstoke
Town Hall Market, Wed., Sat. New Market Place, Wed., Sat.
Both good for fruit and vegetables. There is also a WI market in Moose Hall, Church Street, Fri., 9.30-11.00.

Bishops Waltham
Bishops Waltham Square, WI market stall, Fri. 8.30-12.30.

Botley
Market Hall, WI market stall, Fri. 9.00-12.00.

Fareham
Centre Car Park, Mon. a.m.
Some fruit and vegetables, but chiefly a good source of supply for meat and fish.

Farnborough
Adjacent to the shopping precinct. Tuesday.
Fruit and vegetables good value and generally very fresh.

Gosport
Tuesday. Some fruit and vegetables, but buy with care. Better value for fish (Berry's) and meat (Yeo's).

Havant
WI market, United Reformed Church Hall, Elm Lane, Fri. 9.30-12.30.

Hayling Island
Seasonal WI market, Congregational Church Hut, Hollow Lane, Fri. 10.00-12.00.

Lymington
WI market, Community Centre, New Street, Fri. 10.00-12.00.

Petersfield
Petersfield Shopping Centre, Wed., Sat.
Fruit, fish and dairy produce worth shopping for. Also, a WI market, St. Peters Church Hall, Fri. 10.00-12.00.

Ringwood
WI market, Ebenezer Hall, Greyfriars, Wed. 8.30-11.30.

Romsey
WI market, Abbey Congregational Hall, Fri. 9.00-12.00.

Titchfield
WI market, St. Peters Parish Hall, Fri. 10.00-12.00.

Winchester
WI market, Holy Trinity Church Hall, Upper Brook Street, Fri. 9.00-12.30.

HEREFORDSHIRE

Bromyard
WI market, Public Hall, New Road, Thurs. 9.30-12.00.

Hereford
Cattle Market (Wed.), Butter Market (most weekdays). The latter especially for fruit, vegetables, cheese, meat, and free-range eggs. Also a WI market stall, St. Peters Church House, Fri. 8.30-10.30.

Kington
WI market, 1 High Street, Fri. 11.00-12.15.

Ledbury
WI market, St. Katherines Hall, Fri. 10.00-12.00.

Leominster
WI market, Liberal Rooms, School Lane, Fri. 9.30-1.00.

Ross-on-Wye
WI market, Merton Annexe, Edde Cross Street, Sat. 8.30-12.00.

South Wye
WI market, St. Martins Church Hall, Ross Road, Fri. 2.00-3.30.

HERTFORDSHIRE

Barnet
WI market, High Street, Sat. 8.30-12.30.

Berkhampstead
Town Hall, WI market, Sat. 8.00-12.00.

Bishop Stortford
Palmers Lane, Tues., Thurs., Fri., Sat. WI market, 8.00-4.00.

Hatfield
WI market (part of a larger general market), Market Place, Queensway, Sat. 8.30-4.30.

Hemel Hampstead
Market Place, Thurs., Fri., Sat. Particularly worth visiting for fruit and vegetables.

Hitchin
Tues., Sat. Near St. Mary's Church.
Fresh, locally grown fruit and vegetables, also good for dairy produce. A WI market is held every Saturday from 8.30 to 1.00 in West Alley, Hitchin Arcade.

Royston
The Corn Exchange, Fish Hill. WI market stall Wed. (9.00-12.00), Sat. (8.30-12.00).

St. Albans
St. Peters Street, Market Square, Wed., Sat.
Fruit and vegetables. WI market stall, Sat. 7.30-4.30.

Watford
The Shrubbery, Tues., Fri., Sat. Fruit and vegetables, fresh farm produce in general, fish and meat also excellent buys.

Hertford
Covered and open air markets, daily. Fruit and vegetables, fish, meat.

KENT

Aperfield
WI market, WI Hall, Biggin Hill, Fri. 10.15-11.15.

Ashford
General Market, with WI market stall, Tues., Fri. 8.30-12.00.

Borough Green
WI market, Village Hall, Thurs. 2.15-4.00.

Bromley
Station Road, Thurs.
Fruit particularly good, less so the choice and quality of vegetables.

Canterbury
Market Hall. WI market stall in market, Wed. 8.30-12.30.

Lowe's of Canterbury, 21 The Borough.
More than a hundred years old, general groceries and seasonal stocks of locally produced fruit and vegetables.

Dartford
WI market, The Leisure Club, Lowfield Street, Fri. 10.00-11.30.

Dartford Health Food Centre, 86 Dartmouth Road.
Wide delicatessen stock which includes fresh locally (organically) grown fruit and vegetables.

Dover
WI market, Wesley Hall, Folkestone Road, Thurs. 9.30-11.45.

Faversham
WI market, The Minor Hall, The Institute, East Street, Wed. (9.15-11.30), Fri. (2.15-4.30).

Folkestone
WI market, RC Church Hall, Guildhall Street, Fri. 9.30-11.30.

'Deva', 12 Church Street.
Apples from Little Densole Farm, fresh vegetables from Goldsmiths Farm in the Alkham Valley, fresh herbs in season. Well worth a visit.

Hawkhurst
WI market, Dunks Room, Rye Road, Thurs. 10.00-11.30.

Herne Bay
Town Centre, Saturday. Fruit and vegetables good.

Ide Hill
Seasonal WI market, Village Hall, Wed. 11.00-1.00.

Maidstone
WI market, Dunk Memorial Hall, Church Street, Fri. 8.15-11.00.

Orpington
WI market, next to the multi-storey car park. Fri. 9.45-12.00.

Often spectacularly good fresh fruit and vegetables, although supplies are not continuous.

Pembury
WI market, Village Hall, Fri. 10.30-11.30.

Sandwich
Market Place, WI market, Thurs. 9.00-1.00.

Sevenoaks
WI market, Cornwall Hall, The Drive, Fri. 10.00-12.30.
The town market is on Wednesday, and is also a good market to shop for fruit and vegetables in, although it is said that the fish is the best of all bargains (Jean's Fish Bar).

Sittingbourne
WI market, Brenchley House, High Street, Fri. 9.15-12.00.

Tonbridge
Large WI market, Scouts HQ, River Walk, Fri. 10.15-12.00, for fruit and vegetables, eggs, preserves and delicious home-baked cakes.

Tunbridge Wells
WI market, Christ Church Hall, High Street, Tues. 10.15-12.00.

LANCASHIRE

Ashton-under-Lyne
Town Hall. Closed Tuesday.
Particularly good for fruit and vegetables and — surprisingly — coffee.

Bolton
Ashburner Street. Tues., Thurs., Sat. Fruit and vegetables good, but look out also for dairy produce, including cheeses, cooked meats, oat cakes (a local speciality) and shellfish in the Friday fish market.

Bury
Shopping precinct. Wed., Fri., Sat. Wide selection of greengroceries. While in the market, try and sample some of the Cheshire and Lancashire cheeses available. Worth stopping at the fishmonger's and butcher's stalls, which are of unusually high quality.

Chorley
Tues., Fri., Sat. One greengrocer's stall in particular offers an extremely wide range of fresh produce. Most of the other fruit and vegetable stalls are well worth patronising, as standards are high.

Clitheroe
WI market, St. Mary's Lower Hall, York Street, Tues. 10.30-12.00.

C. R. Hargreaves and Sons Ltd., 40-48 Parson Lane.
Old established grocers specialising in fruit and vegetables produced from local farms.

Denton
Market Square, Fri., Sat. Fruit and vegetables.

Garstang
WI market, Oddfellows Hall, Croston Road, Thurs. 10.30-12.00.

Grange-over-Sands
WI market, St. Johns Ambulance HQ, Fernleigh Road, Fri. 10.00-12.00.

Lancaster
Central shopping area. Monday-Saturday.
Particularly good for fresh fruit and vegetables, meat and fish.

Lea
WI market, Methodist Hall, Birksdale Drive, Tues. 10.15-11.45.

Kirkham
WI market, United Reformed Church Hall, Thurs. 10.00-12.00.

The second market in Kirkham is a privately-owned, open air market, with one stall for each type of produce, of which fruit and vegetables are naturally included. The cheese and fish stalls are considered to be excellent.

Oldham
Town Centre, Mon., Fri., Sat.
Fruit and vegetables (although quality inconsistent) and dairy produce.

Ormskirk
Street market, shopping centre, Thurs., Sat.
Fruit and vegetables good, fish excellent.

Preston
Open air and covered markets, town centre.
Fruit and vegetables in the covered market (open Mon.-Sat., closed Thurs., p.m.) expensive but good.

Rochdale
Of the three markets in Oldham, the covered market is generally considered to offer better value and higher quality. Fruit and vegetables, fish, cheeses, poultry and tripe (!).

Wigan
Covered daily market. Fruit and vegetables; look out also for local shellfish. cheese.

Warrington
Market Hall, Town Centre. Monday to Saturday, closing early Thursday.
Highly commended market, with an unusually high number of delicatessen-type stalls. Fruit and vegetables available (and very good) together with very un-market delicacies such as game and hare (in season), home-cured bacon, cheeses, fish, poultry and freshly baked bread.

Ulverston
Open and covered markets. Town Centre. Wide range of fruit and vegetable stalls. Also good for fish, cheese.

WI market, Coronation Hall, County Square, Thurs. 10.00-11.45.

LEICESTERSHIRE/RUTLAND

Ashby
High Street, Thursday.
Fruit and vegetables, meat, fish and eggs all worth buying.

Hinckley
WI market, Borough Congregational Hall, Fri. 10.00-11.30.

Leicester
Adjacent to Corn Exchange, Wed., Fri., Sat.
Unusually wide range of fruit and vegetables (the market caters to the needs of Leicester's large Indian and Pakistani communities), good buys in fish, cheese and meat.

Loughborough
Thurs., Sat. Fruit and vegetables good value. Worth shopping in the market for fish and poultry, cheese.

Loughborough also has a seasonal WI market at the Woodgate Baptist Schoolroom on Thursdays, 10.30-11.30.

Taylor's, 20-30 Derby Square, sells vegetables in season from the Longford Organic Farm.

Lutterworth
Seasonal WI market, Town Hall, Thurs. 10.00-11.30.

Market Harborough
Three markets, of which the food market (Tuesday, Sat.) sells fruit and vege-

tables, meat, fish, bread, cheese and bacon — all of which are worth visiting the market for.

Melton Mowbray
Town Centre, Tues., Sat. Fruit and vegetables, cheese good buys.

Seasonal WI market, Gloucester House, Park Road, Tues. 10.00-11.30.

Oakham
WI market, Victoria Hall, Fri. 10.00-12.00.

Uppingham
Seasonal WI market, Methodist School Room, Orange Street, Fri. 10.00-11.30.

LINCOLNSHIRE

Alford
Town Centre, Tues., Sat.
Fruit, vegetables (and fish — from the Grimsby Fish Stall, which sells crabs, cockles in season).

Bourne
WI market stall, Market Square, Sat. 8.30-12.00.

Grantham
WI market, Congregational Church Hall, Castlegate, Fri. 10.30-12.00.

Immingham
Council Market, WI market stall, Fri. 9.00 onwards.

Lincoln
Butter Market, Sincil Street. WI market stall, Fri. 8.30-12.30.

Stamford
Town market, Fri., Sat. Fruit and vegetables, fish and cheese.

WI market, Assembly Rooms, Fri. 10.00-11.30.

MONMOUTHSHIRE

Abergavenny
Market Hall, Tues., Sat. (May-Sept. only).
Fruit and vegetables (Nuth's stall in particular); fish, meat. home-cured bacon, cheese also worth sampling. WI market stall on Tues., Fri. in the mornings.

Chepstow
WI market, Manor Grill, Fri. 9.00-11.30.

Monmouth
Shire Hall, Agincourt Square, WI market, Fri. 8.00-12.00.

Newport
Market Hall, Mon.-Sat. Fruit, vegetables, fish.
WI market stall, Market Hall Gallery, Fri. 7.00-2.00.

Blackwood
WI market, Ambulance Hall, Fri. 10.00-12.00.

Usk
WI market, Nag's Head, The Square, Thurs. 9.30-11.30.

MONTGOMERYSHIRE

Newtown
Market Hall. WI market stall in the market, Fri. (12.00-4.30); Sat. (9.00-1.30).

Welshpool
Market Hall. WI market stall in the market, Sat. 8.00-1.00.

NORFOLK

Dereham
Town Square, Fri. Locally grown fruit and vegetables, fresh poultry, fish.

Also, a WI market, Wellington Road, East Dereham, Fri. 9.30-12.00.

Fakenham
WI market in The Old Cattle Market, Thurs. 10.00-12.30.

Kings Lynn
Town Square, Tuesday.
Fruit and vegetables (Hardy's of Wisbech in particular), fish (Burgess of Lincoln).

Norwich
Market Square, Tues.-Sat.
Fruit and vegetables (Seamans usually have an extremely wide choice of fresh vegetables), fish and sea food. WI market stall (Nos. 67, 68), Thurs. 9.00-12.30.

Taylor's, 15 Lower Goat Lane, usually has fresh, organically grown vegetables and culinary herbs, in season.

Stalham
Maid's Head. Market auction, Tues.
Fresh local produce, including fruit and vegetables, dairy produce.

Watton
WI market, Methodist Hall, High Street, Wed. 9.00-12.00.

NORTHAMPTONSHIRE

Brackley
Market Place, WI market stall, Fri. 8.00-1.00.

Kettering
Market Square, WI market stall, Fri. 9.30-12.00.

Northampton
Market Square, Town Centre, Wed., Fri., Sat. Fruit and vegetables – and fish, pork meat.

Towcester
WI market, Saracen's Head Hotel, Fri. 2.00-4.00.

NORTHUMBERLAND

Alnwick
Fish Market. Seasonal WI market stall, Fri. 9.30-11.00.

Berwick-on-Tweed
Butter Market, Town Hall. Seasonal WI market stall, Wed. 9.30-12.30.

Hexham
Market Place, Tues. Fruit and vegetables.

Also, a WI market, Tues., Tynedale Room, County Hotel, 10.30-12.00.

Rothbury
Seasonal WI market, The Shop, Commercial Building, Fri. 9.30-12.00.

Newcastle-upon-Tyne
The Grainger Market, Mon.-Sat.
Greengroceries, meat (Arthur Temple), game (Warner and Hurst), cheese (J. H. Matthews) and fish.

Bigg Market, Tues., Thurs., Sat. Fruit and vegetables high quality.

Whitley Bay
Adjacent to car park. Thurs., Sat. Good for fruit and vegetables.

Wooler
Seasonal WI market, The Path, Sat. 10.00-12.00.

NOTTINGHAMSHIRE

Newark

Town Square, Wed., Sat. Greengroceries, fish, dairy produce, pork. The WI market stall is held in the Butter Market section, Wed. 7.30-2.00.

Nottingham

WI market, YWCA Hall, Shakespeare Street, Fri. 7.45-12.30.

Retford

Town Square, Sat.
Fruit and vegetables, free-range eggs, market garden produce. WI stall, Sat. 8.00-12.00, in the Butter Market nearby.

OXFORDSHIRE

Banbury

WI market stall in Banbury Market, Market Place, Sat. 8.00-12.45.

Burford

WI market, The Tolsey, High Street, Fri. 9.30-12.00.

Chipping Norton

WI market stall, Methodist School Room, West Street, Fri. 9.30-12.00.

Oxford

Open air market, Wed.
Fresh fruit and vegetables, fish (Jones and Co.), eggs, meat (E. Greer's stall particularly worth visiting). Oxford also has a covered market open on weekdays. The WI have a stall there on Wed., and Fri. 8.00-2.30. Also good for tea and freshly roasted coffee, cheeses.

Thame

Country market with locally produced fruit and vegetables, eggs, etc.

Wallingford

WI market, Town Hall, Fri. 9.30-11.30.

Witney

WI market, Palace Cinema, Thurs. 9.00-1.00.

Woodstock

Town Hall, WI market stall, Fri. 9.45-12.30.

PEMBROKESHIRE

Manorbier

Seasonal WI market, Village Hall, Wed. 8.45-12.00.

Milford Haven
WI market, Robert Street, Fri. 8.45-12.00.

Narberth
WI market, WI Hall, Thurs. 9.30-12.00.

St. Davids
WI market, High Street, Thurs. 10.00 onwards.

Tenby
The Market, Frog Street. WI market stall there, Fri. 9.45-11.45.

SHROPSHIRE

Ellesmere
Market Hall, WI market stall there, Tues. 9.00-12.30.

Ludlow
Town Hall. WI market stall, Sat. 8.00-2.00.

Market Drayton
Covered Market Hall, Cheshire Street. WI market held there, Wed. 9.00-2.00.

Newport
Market Hall. WI market stall, Fri. 8.30-1.30.

Oswestry
Powys Hall Market, Wed., Sat. Fruit, vegetables and a good selection of cheeses. WI market stall in the market, on both days, 8.30-2.30.

Wholefood Shop and Bakery. As the name implies, basically a whole food shop, but with a wide variety of fresh, locally grown fruit, vegetables and herbs, in season.

Shrewsbury
General Market Hall. WI market stall in the market, Sat. 8.00-2.00.

Wellington
Market Hall. Thurs., Sat. Also, WI market stall, Thurs. 8.00-2.00.

Whitchurch
New Market Hall. WI market stall, Fri. 8.30-1.00.

SOMERSET

Bath
General market daily.

WI market, Rivers Street, Fri. 10.30-1.30.

Bridgwater
General market daily.

WI market, 2a Angel Crescent, Fri. 8.30-3.00.

Bristol
St. Nicholas Market, Mon.-Sat. Fruit, vegetables and general market produce.

Blackwell
WI market, WI Hall, Cross Roads, Fri. 8.30-12.00.

Burnham-on-Sea
Princess Hall. WI market stall, Fri. 8.30-12.00.

Clevedon
St. Johns Hall, Hillside Road, WI market, Fri. 10.30-12.00.

Frome
WI market, 6 Catherine Road, Fri. (9.30-4.30), Sat. (9.00-11.30).

Ilminster
WI market, Dolphin Hotel, Wed. 10.00-12.00.

Nailsea
WI market, Toc H Hall, Silver Street, Fri. 10.00-11.30.

Portishead
WI market, Church Hall, Combe Road, Fri. 11.00-12.00.

Shepton Mallet
The Peter Street Rooms, WI market, Fri. 10.00-12.00.

Taunton
General market, Sat.

WI market, Bath Place, Fri. 8.30-3.00, also Wed.

Wellington
Community Centre, White Horse Lane, WI market, Fri. 10.00-12.00.

Wells
The Little Theatre, Chamberlain Street, WI market, 9.30-11.30. Small market in town centre, Wed., Sat.

Wincanton
WI market, White Horse Hotel, Fri. 10.00-12.00.

Yeovil
General Market, Fri.

WI market, Princes Street, Wed., Fri. 8.30-5.00.

STAFFORDSHIRE

Burton-on-Trent
Market Place. Thurs., Sat.
Fruit and vegetables, eggs, cheese and other general farm products. WI market stall on Thurs., in the market hall, 7.30-1.00.

Lichfirled
Market Place. WI market stall, Fri. 8.30-1.30.

Stafford
Town Centre. Tues., Fri., Sat.
Fruit, vegetables, fish and cheese all worth shopping for in the market.

Wolverhampton
Town Centre (near car park). Tues., Wed., Fri., Sat.
Fruit and vegetables worth buying in the market, as the town's greengrocers seem to have a dismal track record on quality.

SUFFOLK

Bury St. Edmunds
Street Market. Wed., Sat. Locally grown fruit and vegetables.

WI market, 9 Hatter Street, Tues., Wed., Fri. 9.00-1.00, Sat. 9.00-12.00.

Clare
Town Hall, Market Square. WI market stall, Fri. 10.00-1.00.

Eye
WI market, Assembly Rooms, White Lion Hotel, Wed. 8.30-12.00.

Stowmarket
WI market, British Legion Hall, Tavern Street, Thurs. 8.45-12.00.

Ipswich
Marno's, 14 Nicholas Street.
Wide range of fairly unusual vegetables, some organically grown.

Saxmundham
Rendham Stores, Rendham.
Fresh, locally grown fruit and vegetables in season.

Sudbury
Town Centre. Thurs., Sat.
Fruit and vegetables (from Ben Clark in particular), fresh fish on Thursday (Haslam's), eggs and poultry.

SURREY

Croydon
Surrey Street. Mon.-Sat.
Fruit and vegetables, delicatessen produce, eggs and cheese all worth shopping for in the market. For fruit, also worth visiting the Pure Food Company, 100 High Street.

Coulsdon and Purley
WI market, South London Harriers Hall, Brighton Road, Fri. 11.00-12.30.

Dorking
WI market, St. Martins Church Hall, Fri. 10.00-12.00.

Epsom
Town Centre. Sat.
Fruit, vegetables and fish (particularly shellfish).

Farnham
WI market, Castle Street, Fri. 9.00-2.00.

Godalming
WI market, Congregational Hall, Bridge Street, Fri. 8.30-11.30.

Also worth visiting the Losely Farm Shop, Crown Court, 44 High Street, for fruit (and a number of other types of farm produce) from the shop's own farm.

Guildford
Two town markets: North Street (Fri., Sat.), good for fruit and vegetables (visit Pratts and Harveys stalls); Slyfield Market (Wed.), also good for fruit and vegetables.

WI market, Merrow Village Hall, Fri. 9.30-11.30.

Cranks, 35 Castle Street, sell fresh fruit and vegetables from Loseley Park (see Godalming).

Leatherhead
WI market, Scout Hall, Queen Anne's Terrace, Fri. 10.300-11.30.

Also worth visiting: Leatherhead Whole Food Shop, 34 High Street, who sell fresh fruit from Kent, vegetables from Bury Hill Nurseries and fresh herbs in season.

Ockley
W. A. Carpenter Provision Stores.
Fresh fruit and vegetables from Godalming Farms. The added bonus of a good many other delights, including home-cooked hams, dairy produce, free-range eggs.

Reigate
WI market, Methodist School Room, Fri. 9.30-12.00.

Woking
Town market on a new site. Fri., Sat. Fruit, vegetables and eggs.

SUSSEX

Battle
WI market, FOG Hall, St. Mary's Church, Fri. 10.00-11.45.

Bamber
Seasonal WI market, St. Mary's Lodge, High Street, Thurs. 3.00-5.00.

Burwash
WI market, Village Hall, Tues. 10.30-12.00.

Chichester
Butter Market, North Street, Tues.-Sat. WI stall there, on all five days, 8.30-3.30.

Crowborough
WI market, WI Market Hut, Eridge Road, Fri. 8.00-12.00.

Eastbourne
Seasonal WI market, Foresters Hall, Langney Road, Fri. 10.30-11.15.

Hailsham
WI market, RC Hall, South Road, Fri. 9.45-11.45.

Hastings
WI market, All Saints Church Hall, Old Town, Fri. 10.00-12.00.

Henfield
Seasonal WI market, High Street, Sat. 8.00-12.00.

Horsham
WI market, Piries Place, Carfax, Fri. 9.00-12.30.

Lindfield
WI market, King Edward Hall, High Street, Tues. 9.00-11.00.

Mayfield
WI market, Memorial Hall Car Park, Fri. 10.00-11.30.

Midhurst
WI market, Grange Road, Car Park, Fri. 9.00-12.30.

Newick
Newick Village Hall, WI market, Fri. 10.00 onwards.

Rye

WI market, Community Centre, Conduit Hill, Fri. 10.00-11.30.

Selsey

Seasonal WI market, Barn at rear of Fire Station, Tues. 10.00-12.00.

Storrington

WI market, Village Hall, West Street, Fri. 8.30-12.00.

Winchelsea

Seasonal WI market, Castle Street, Fri. 9.00-12.00.

WARWICKSHIRE

Alcester

WI market, 39a High Street, Fri. 8.30-1.00.

Coleshill

WI market, The Parish Room, High Street, Fri. 9.30-11.45.

Coventry

Town Centre, Wed., Fri., Sat.
Fruit and vegetables good — also meat (and game in season), free-range eggs, and other dairy produce.

Kineton

WI market, WI Hall, Sat. 10.30-11.30.

Leamington Spa

WI market, Oddfellows Hall, Warwick Street, Fri. 9.00-12.00.

Rugby

Street market in Railway Terrace, Gas Street. Sat., Mon. a.m.
Fruit and vegetables.

Also, the WI market, Thurs. 9.30-11.30, Brotherhood Hall, Castle Street.

Shipston-on-Stour

WI market, Townsend Hall, Sheep Street, Sat. 9.15-11.30.

Southam

WI market, Youth Centre, Market Hill, Fri. 2.00-4.00.

Stratford-on-Avon

Rother Street, Fri.
Fruit and vegetables, poultry, fish and cheese all worth shopping for in the market.

WESTMORLAND

Ambleside
Seasonal WI market, YMCA, St. Mary's Lane, Fri. 9.30-11.30.

Kendal
WI market, YMCA, Strickland Gate, Fri. 10.30-12.00.

Milnthorpe
Market Square, WI market stall, Church Hall (Market Square), Fri. 10.00-11.30.

Sedbergh
WI market, British Legion Room, Kings Yard, Fri. 10.30-11.45.

WILTSHIRE

Chippenham
WI market, Neeld Hall, Fri. 8.00-3.00.

Devizes
Market Square, Thurs., Sat. WI market stall in the market, Thurs. 8.30-2.30.

Marlborough
General Market, Wed., Sat.

WI market, High Street, Sat. 8.00-12.00.

Melksham
WI market stall in the market, Thurs. 9.30-1.00.

Salisbury
General Market, Tues., Sat. WI have a stall in the market, Sat. 8.00-4.00. Good for fruit and vegetables, fish, meat.

Swindon
General market daily.

WI market, 188 Victoria Road, Fri. 8.15-12.00.

Trowbridge
Market Hall, Tues., Sat. WI stall there, Sat. 8.30-1.00.

WORCESTERSHIRE

Bredon Hill
WI market, The Garden House, New Road, Eckington, Fri. 9.30-12.00.

Bromsgrove
Market Hall. WI stall there on Fri. 9.30-12.30, and in the summer season also on

Tues., same times.

Droitwich
WI market, Sacred Heart Parish Room, Worcester Road, Fri. 9.30-11.30.

Also worth visiting: Prana Wholefoods, 6 High Street, who sell fresh fruit and vegetables from their own farm.

Evesham
WI market, Bewdley Street, Fri. 9.00-12.00.

Great Malvern
WI market, Lytleton Rooms, Church Street, Fri. 9.00-12.00.

Kidderminster
Market Hall, Worcester Street, WI stall, Thurs. 8.30-3.30.

Redditch
Royal Square Open Market, Tues., Thurs., Sat.
Fruit and vegetables, cooked meats, bacon. WI stall in the market, Tues. 9.00-1.30.

Stourbridge
Market Hall, WI stall, Fri. 8.30-5.30.

Tenbury Wells
WI market, The Pump Room, Tues. 9.30-2.00.

Worcester
WI market, St. Albans Church Hall, Deansway, Fri. 9.00-12.30.

YORKSHIRE

Barnsley
Charter Hall Market, Kendray Market. Wed., Fri., Sat.
Fruit and vegetables particularly good.

Beverley
Open air market, town centre. Recommended for fruit and vegetables.

Bradford
Rawson Place Market, Mon.-Sat.
Fruit and vegetables, meat (cheaper and better than elsewhere in town), fish and cheese.

Kirkgate Market, Mon.-Sat.
Some fruit and vegetables, but on the whole better for things like cakes, bread, fresh herbs.

John Street Market. Mon.-Sat.
Again, some fruit and vegetables, but on the whole not as good as Rawson Place. Still worth visiting for coffee (Collinson's) and delicatessen foods.

Doncaster
Town Centre, Tues., Fri., Sat.
Highly recommended for fruit and vegetables, fish, cheese, free-range eggs.

Dewsbury
Open air market, town centre. Wed., Sat.
Good for greengroceries in general, and cheese.

Huddersfield
Mondays. Fruit and vegetables a very good buy – better and cheaper than elsewhere in town.

Leeds
Tues., Fri., Sat. Good for fruit and vegetables, fish, meat and poultry.

Northallerton
Sat., Wed. Especially good for fruit and vegetables – locally grown and more colourful imports (Hebdon and Sons for local produce).

Ripon
Town Square. Thurs., Sat.
Fruit and vegetables, most of them fresh, locally grown and very good.

Sheffield
Castle Market, Mon.-Sat. (Closed Thurs.).
Fruit and vegetables (Marsh, Coates and Hinchliffe, in particular), meat, fish.

Sheaf Market, opposite Castle Market. Tues., Fri., Sat.
Good for fruit and vegetables.

Skipton
Open air market, main street, Wed., Sat. Good choice of fruit and vegetables.

Wakefield
Open market, next to main shopping centre, Mon., Fri., Sat.
Extremely good fruit and vegetables, which have ousted the more established greengrocers in the town.

York
Newgate, Mon. (early closing)-Sat.
Fruit and vegetables, fish – and delicious home-made cakes.

London Markets

Berwick Street Market, W1. Mon.-Sat. Possibly the best fruit and vegetable market in London, with an enormous choice, good quality and value.

Brixton Market, SW9. Mon.-Sat., early closing Wed. Atalantic Road. Wide variety of fruit and vegetables (and – because of the West Indian community it serves – a likely hunting ground for exotica).

Chapel Street Market, N1. Tues.-Sun. Good general food market, with enormous number of fruit and vegetable stalls.

Church Street Market, NW8. Only half of the market devoted to foodstuffs, but worth visiting for fruit and vegetables.

The Cut Market, SE1. Mon.-Sat. Basic greengroceries.

Deptford Market, Douglas Way, SE8. Fri., Sat. Generally reliable fruit and vegetable stalls.

East Street Market, Walworth Road, SE17. Open all week. Good for fruits and vegetables (and just about anything else you can think of!).

Hessel Street Market, E1. Mon.-Fri. Vegetables, fresh herbs, delicatessen foods.

Inverness Street Market, NW1, Mon.-Sat. (early closing Thurs.). Small, but good for fruit, vegetables and dairy produce.

Kingsland Road Market, E8. Mon.-Sat. (Thurs. early closing) Some greengroceries. Good East End market.

Leather Lane Market, EC1. Lunchtime opening, standard, but generally good fruit and vegetable stalls.

North End Road Market, SW6. Usually good (and very cheap) fruit and vegetables.

Northcote Road Market, SW11. Mon.-Sat. (early closing Wed.) Almost entirely fruit and vegetables.

Portobello Road, W10. Mon.-Sat. (early closing Wed.) Hidden amongst all the other stalls and shops are some very good fruit and vegetable stalls.

Shepherds Bush Market, W12. Wed., Fri., Sat. Occasionally good for greengroceries in general, but less likely as a source of consistently good food.

Wentworth Street Market, E1. Mon.-Fri. Generally good for fruit and vegetables.

Whitecross Street Market, EC1. Open all week, but fruit and vegetables only really worth shopping for on Friday.

Mail Order Fruit and Vegetables

Most fruits and vegetables don't take kindly to postal delivery — for obvious reasons. The major exceptions are apples and pears, which can be ordered in season from the following suppliers:

B. A. Dench, Ringden Farm, Hurst Green, Etchingham, Sussex.

Blackmoor Estate Ltd., Blackmoor, Liss, Hants.

Executive Economy Ltd., Owlett Farm, Lamberhurst, Kent.

Leigh Sinton Farm Ltd., Leigh Sinton, Malvern, Worcs.

Bexon Manor Fruit Farm, Bregdar, Sittingbourne, Kent.

Leckford Estate Ltd., The Old Rectory, Leckford, Stockbridge, Hants.

F. Bridgeland, Longbrooks Farm, Brenchley, Kent.

Norwoods Fruit Farm, Ticehirst, Wadhurst, Sussex.

P. L. Barker, Esq., Dward Pyramids, Wood Farm, Gamlingay, Nr. Saney, Beds.

Broomfields, Holt Heath, Worcester.

Giles Tuker Ltd., Butts Green Orchards, Danbury, Essex.

Some of the above suppliers operate a back-up guarantee if fruit is not up to standard on arrival, but in order to take advantage of this, and to be fair to the growers, any substandard fruit should be returned immediately if there is any cause for complaint.

One firm, in addition, will mail fruit anywhere, provided the fruit is available and more or less in season. They usually offer this as a service comparable to Interflora, and not as a specifically mail order service: Fruit Relay Service, 238 Green Lanes, London N13 5TU (Tel: 01 882 1074). Fortnum and Mason, and one or two of the food halls in London's larger department stores will mail hampers of fruit and vegetables, in season, to destinations throughout the UK.

For those who are interested in organically grown fruit and vegetables, the three associations listed below can supply directories of farmers and suppliers:

The Soil Association, Walnut Tree Manor, Haughley, Suffolk.

The Henry Doubleday Research Association, 22 Convent Lane, Braintree, Essex.

The Organic Food Service, Churston Ferrers, South Devon.

HERBS AND SPICES

Culinary herbs and spices have a long and colourful history, most of it, sadly, quite beyond the scope of a brief introduction. It is of interest to note, however, that we now use herbs and spices in much the same way that they were used in the fifteenth century, and possibly earlier -- although probably for very different reasons! Then, spices in particular were a luxury and their use was probably restricted to those who could afford to pay for variation and flavour in an otherwise drearily monotonous diet. The poor used what they could find in the way of culinary herbs, or went without, enduring their salted meat and boiled fish without adornment.

In the seventeenth and eighteenth centuries, spices and herbs were less frequently added directly to the food whilst cooking. They were more usually mixed and brewed with other ingredients to produce 'store sauces' – better able to withstand the rigours of the long sea voyages for which they were originally used by the East India traders. By the nineteenth century, sauces had become so much a part of popular taste that they were practically the only commonly used method for spicing foods. Families produced their own 'table sauces', frequently rather horrific ones, and these were the forerunners of the ubiquitous brown sauces and ketchups of today.

It has only been in comparatively recent times that herbs and spices have again been used as a direct flavouring. Quite why habits change so completely is something of a mystery – and one that I am quite happy to let others solve. Far more important is the fact that we are learning once again to appreciate, experiment, improvise and enjoy the great variety of herbs and spices commonly available, and to search out newer or less familiar ones.

SOURCES OF SUPPLY

The following suppliers have been divided into three categories. The first section deals with those shops carrying a wider than normal range of spices and herbs, most of them catering for personal shoppers only. The second section lists mail order suppliers. Obviously, for the most part they can only supply dried herbs, although one or two of them are prepared to send fresh herbs when supplies and conditions permit. The final section lists those herb gardens and herbal specialists supplying herb plants. They will advise on the suitability of various herbs, the conditions most favoured and the results to be expected, and are well worth approaching if you can spare even the smallest of spaces in which to grow your own — they are invariably fresher, and very much prettier than their dried counterparts! A short list of specialist mustards appears at the end of the section.

Shops

The following shops, listed alphabetically by town, carry a wider than average range of herbs and spices:

SUNVITA HERBAL REMEDIES

150 Victoria Road, Aldershot, Hampshire.

KITCHEN 46

46 Kingsbury, Aylesbury, Bucks.

BRISTOL GUILD OF APPLIED ARTS

68 Park Street, Bristol 1. Tel: 0272 25548.

KITCHENS

4 Waterloo Street, Clifton, Bristol 8. Tel: 0272 39848. And at
167 Whiteladies Road, Clifton, Bristol 8. Tel: 0272 39614.

SPICE OF LIFE

87 Station Road, Birchington, Margate, Kent.

THE KITCHEN SHOP

1a Carter Street, Blackpool.

GERARD HOUSE

736b Christchurch Road, Boscombe, Hampshire (also at 2a Browning Avenue, Boscombe).

THE OLD BAKEHOUSE

3 Sherborne Street, Bourton-on-the-Water, Gloucestershire.

JOHN DAY AND SONS (HERBALISTS)

90 Kirkgate Market, Bradford, Yorkshire.

A traditional herbalist's shop, with a wide range of culinary herbs.

CATERHAM HEALTH FOODS

81 Croydon Road, Caterham, Surrey CR3 6PD.

SPEARINGS

Dedham, nr. Colchester, Essex.

LAWS HERBAL SUPPLIES

270 High Street, Gateshead, Durham.

THE WHEATSHEAF

107 High Street, Great Missenden, Buckinghamshire.

THE PEPPERMILL

Halesowen, Worcestershire.

ALDRINGHAM CRAFT MARKET

14 Upper Brook Street, Ipswich, Suffolk.

LOVETT FLINT

22 Mill Street, Kidderminster, Worcestershire.

BALDWINS

173 Walworth Road, London SE17. Tel: 01 703 5550.
Old fashioned herbalist, with over 200 varieties of dried herbs in stock. Can supply mail order customers.

BOMBAY EMPORIUM LTD.

70 Grafton Way, London W1. Tel: 01 387 4514.
Vast range of curry spices, chutneys, pickles and condiments. Can supply mail order customers, as well as personal shoppers.

CULPEPERS

21 Bruton Street, London W1X 1DA. Tel: 01 629 4559.

59 Ebury Street, London SW1 0NZ. Tel: 01 730 0361/2.

9 Flask Walk, London NW3. Tel: 01 794 7263.

All three London branches of Culpepers sell a good range of culinary herbs and spices. The Flask Walk branch also sells herb plants.

FALCON HERBAL

44 Falcon Road, London SW11. Tel: 01 228 8024.
One hundred and fifty varieties of herbs, a good many of them culinary.

HAELAN CENTRE

39 Park Road, London N8. Tel: 01 340 4258.
Some herb plants, and 300 varieties of dried herbs.

HARRODS

Knightsbridge, London SW1. Tel: 01 730 1234.

JACKSONS

171 Piccadilly, London W1. Tel: 01 493 1033.

6a Sloane Street, London SW1. Tel: 01 235 9233.

24 Kendal Street, Hyde Park, London W2. Tel: 01 262 9122.

SESAME

128 Regents Park Road, London NW1. Tel: 01 586 3779.

THE KITCHENER

6 Monmow Street, Monmouth.

BURTONS

Smith Row, Nottingham.

CULPEPERS

14 Bridewell Alley, Norwich.

MAWSONS

57 George Street, Oldham, Lancashire.

THE HERB SHOP

Pentrevoelas, Denbighshire, North Wales.

DOROTHY WARD

Skipton, Yorkshire.

QUANTUM

George Street, Saffron Walden, Essex.

DARTINGTON HALL SHOP

Totnes, Devon.

SCOTLAND

VALVONA AND CROLLA LTD.

19 Elm Row, Edinburgh 7.

HENDERSONS LTD.

Sauchiehall Street, Glasgow.

THE ITALIAN WAREHOUSE

High Street, Perth.

Mail Order Suppliers

CULPEPERS

59 Ebury Street, London SW1. Tel: 01 730 0361.
Whole herbs (in sprig or leaf), herb and spice blends, and selected spices available by post.

YOUNG AND SAUNDERS LTD.

5 Queensferry Street, Edinburgh EH2 4PD.
Enormous selection of herbs and spices available by mail order, mainly from three brand-name ranges: French's, Pannet and Neden, Spice Island. Also available: green peppercorns, dried root ginger, and natural and coarse salt.

HABITAT

Mail Order Department, Hithercroft Road, Wallingford, Berkshire.
A small range of herbs and spices available by mail order, including a 'set' of curry spices, ½ lb. bags of whole black peppercorns, green peppercorns, natural and coarse salt, saffron, Maldon sea salt, crystal salt.

Plants (Herbs)

The following suppliers will post herb plants to mail order customers. They can also supply personal shoppers. Write or phone for the various catalogues available.

STOKE LACEY HERB FARM

Bromyard, Herefordshire. Tel: Burley Gate 232.

E. AND A. EVETTS

Ashfields Herb Nursery, Hinstock, Market Drayton, Shropshire.
Tel: Sambrook 392.

TUMBLERS BOTTOM HERB FARM

Kilmersdon, Radstock, Somerset. Tel: Radstock 3452.

THE HERB FARM

Broad Oak Road, Canterbury, Kent. Tel: Canterbury 52254.

THE OLD RECTORY HERB GARDEN

Ightham, Kent. Tel: Borough Green 882608.

VALESWOOD HERB FARM

Little Ness, Shropshire. Tel: Baschurch 376.

MUSTARDS

Mustard is very much a commonplace, but it is sometimes difficult to track down alternatives to the ubiquitous English mustard. I have therefore included a short list of specialist suppliers, most of whom, unless indicated otherwise, will be happy to supply any of the mustards by mail order.

THE MUSTARD SHOP

3 Bridewell Alley, Norwich NOR 02H.
Established and run by Colmans, but none the worse for that, as they sell, and will post to those customers unable to get to the shop, a number of mustards not included in their more familiar range. These include their own formulation of German and American mustard and three French mustards: Meaux, Bordeaux and Dijon (all supplied packed in stoneware jars). They have also reformulated their English mustard powders, and in addition to the widely available Double Superfine, they also retail a milder Special Blend and a stronger than normal Genuine Double Superfine.

YOUNG AND SAUNDERS LTD.

5 Queensferry Street, Edinburgh EH2 4PD. Tel: 031 225 6075.
Carry a wide range of Continental mustards, all of which can be supplied by mail order or to personal shoppers: Maille, French Tarragon, Moutarde de Meaux Pommery, Moutarde Blanche, Moutarde Florida, Dijon, Grey Dijon. The usual range of English mustards and mustard powders are also available.

DANFOOD LTD.

37 Raynham Road, Industrial Estate, Bishops Stortford, Herts. Tel: 0279 56399.
Supply (to mail order customers only) the Danish speciality Fiskesennep, a fish mustard.

ROBERT JACKSON

171 Piccadilly, London W1. Tel: 01 493 1033.
Supply (by mail order and to personal shoppers) the best-selling French mustard, Moutarde de Meaux Pommery, packed in stoneware jars. Also available at their branches: 6a Sloane Street, London W1 (Tel: 01 235 9233); 24 Kendal Street, Hyde Park, London W2 (Tel: 01 262 9122); 37-41 Seamoor Road, Bournemouth, Hants.; 37 Mount Ephraim, Tunbridge Wells, Kent; and at Thos. Oakley, 9 George Street, St. Albans, Hertfordshire and Halsey and Sons, Market Place, Hitchin, Herts.

TRADERS

John Street, Colchester, Essex. Tel: 0206 79961.
The shop doesn't operate a mail order service, but is worth visiting for, amongst

other things, their Moutarde Grains de Dijon, which is not widely available elsewhere and definitely worth sampling.

SCHMIDTS LONDON LTD.

33-43 Charlotte Street, London W1. Tel: 01 636 8932.

THE GERMAN FOOD CENTRE

44-46 Knightsbridge, London SW1. Tel: 01 235 5760.

Although neither of the above can supply by mail order, they have a wide range of all sorts of German mustards, and in both cases can advise on other sources of supply elsewhere in the UK for customers unable to reach the London stores.

Sweets

CAKES AND ALE – A BRIEF HISTORY OF THE BAKING OF SWEET BISCUITS, CAKES, PUDDINGS AND PIES IN ENGLAND

Amanda Goodfellow

Cakes and biscuits are a comparatively recent development in the evolution of our food. In the Middle Ages, 'cake' was a general term used to describe a shape – flat, round, smallish – usually of bread, but also of sweetmeats. Seventeenth- and eighteenth-century books are full of receipts for 'clear cakes' of summer fruits. These were made by dissolving a large quantity of sugar in the strained juice of the simmered fruit, then pouring the thick syrup thus made into flat pans to dry gently in a stove. The end result, cut up into pieces, made fruity sweetmeats which could be safely stored through the winter and used perhaps, to round off a good meal, or to add flavour to sauces and syrups.

The *true* ancestors of our modern cakes are those ends of dough, left over after the main batch of loaves had been made, which the baker might enrich with spices, currants, butter, sugar, and later eggs, pat into rounds, and pop into the cooling brick oven after the bread had been taken out. Of this practice our Wigs, Bath Buns, Hot Cross Buns and Lardy Cakes are direct descendants. Wigs were so called because of their shape – the round, enriched bun being cut across and across into 'wigs' (Middle English for 'wedges'). They became popular breakfast fare in the seventeenth century, when the old-fashioned heavy breakfast of ale, cooked meats and bread was replaced among the gentry by a light repast of chocolate or coffee, and spiced buns. Wigs, like Hot Cross Buns which they resemble, became, for some reason, associated with Lent. Pepys mentions that he 'came home to the only Lenten supper I have had of Wiggs and ale'. Perhaps the embellishment of ordinary bread during Lent to make spicy, fruit buns was some kind of compensation for the otherwise monotonous and restricted diet of that period. The cross on a Hot Cross Bun, by the way, is said to be a survival of the pre-Reformation custom of marking all loaves with a cross before they went into the oven to ward off evil spirits that might prevent the bread rising. This practice was abandoned as popish in the seventeenth century and was retained only for that day in the church's year when the symbol of the cross had its greatest significance.

Our early 'cakes', or enriched breads, would have been made with whatever the store-cupboard could provide. The dough was of course raised with 'ale barm' – yeast skimmed from brewing ale, and the only leavening agent then known. Spices, in large variety, were essential to the medieval kitchen, and with them came almonds, sugar, and currants, or 'raisins of Corinth', brought by the spice merchants from Spain and the Levant. Eggs were plentiful, and so were milk, butter and cream – and there would also be supplies of candied fruits. And so the earliest cakes for which recipes can be found are concoctions of these ingredients. Our taste for them survives to this day in the many varieties of fruit cake to which different parts of the country have given their name, such as Norfolk and Dundee; but how Simnel cake came to be so called is rather obscure. In the Middle Ages, 'Simnel' was a light biscuity confection which had to be boiled before being baked. In the late seventeenth century, however, the name was somehow transferred to the rich fruit cake we know which was baked in mid-Lent and taken home by daughters in service to their mothers on Mothering Sunday. Other cakes, of a slightly different nature, which are mentioned in seventeenth-century cook books are Banbury cakes and Scottish Black Bun – both confections rich in dried or candied fruits and encased in pastry. Eccles cake is a later version of Banbury cake.

In the second half of the seventeenth century it was discovered that a number of eggs, vigorously beaten, provided sufficient leavening for a sweet cake, and ale barm, which was troublesome to use and might impart a bitter taste if not carefully prepared, was eventually left out. The size of these early cakes was often enormous and the time specified for the beating of the mixture proportionately long, two hours being not uncommon. One wonders whether so much labour was really necessary, or whether the authors of these receipts were simply careless of the amount of work they ordained since they had servants to do it for them. Here is Lady Grisell Baillie's recipe, dating from the turn of the seventeenth century, for a seed cake – another popular confection, which goes back at least to Tudor times. Quantities have been reduced to a quarter of the amount specified in the original:

> Take 8 oz. butter, beaten soft with the hand; add thereto 8 oz. warm sifted caster sugar and beat together well; then beat in 4 egg yolks, 8 oz. warmed and sifted flour with a quarter pint of warm sack (sherry or white wine), a spoonful of rosewater and a pinch each of mace, nutmeg and cinnamon. Beat the egg whites, leave to stand, and fold in the froth only with ½ oz. of caraway seeds. Turn into a buttered hoop and bake in a quick oven.

I have made this successfully myself, and it only differs from more recent recipes for seed cake in the amount of wine, rosewater and spices it prescribes. Other recipes of the same period often specify the use of caraway comfits, either kneaded into the cake itself, or strewn over the top. Another typical receipt adds, 'If you please to ice it, take the white of one egg, rose water and sugar and three or four grains of Ambergrease. It must be cold before you ice it and if you must, sett it into the oven to harden it.' Both the manufacture of 'comfits' and the icing of cakes emphasise the growing popularity of sugar, and the conspicuous uses to which it was put. Caraway seeds, and 'comfits' (caraway seeds coated in sugar, as our sugared almonds of today) were always to be found in the well-stocked kitchen of the sixteenth, seventeenth and eighteenth centuries, along with the usual spices, rosewater and orange-flower water (much used to scent biscuits and cakes). The exotic musk and ambergrease, popular in Tudor and Stuart times, but always expensive, and used in very small quantities, had more or less disappeared from the English kitchen by the mid-eighteenth century. Sack, also frequently specified, was a dry amber wine from Southern Spain, similar to a dry sherry.

Cakes were large, of course, since households were so large. At this time, late seventeenth and early eighteenth century, such cakes would only have been baked by the wealthy. What most contributed to the universal consumption of cake was the cheapness and availability of sugar, from the end of the seventeenth century, and the adoption of tea-drinking as a national habit. Sugar, up to the Tudor and early Stuart period, had been a luxury which only the very rich could afford. The sweetener commonly used was honey. But sugar, because of its scarcity value, and supposed medicinal properties, had always been sought after. With the opening up of the spice trade with the Far East, and the establishment of sugar plantations in the West Indies in the middle of the seventeenth century, sugar fell in price, and was imported in ever-increasing quantities. In Elizabeth's reign, the average yearly consumption of sugar was one pound a head, a hundred years later, four pounds a head, and by the dawn of the nineteenth century, thirteen pounds a head – in spite of the high food prices then prevailing, for by that time the British had become thoroughly addicted to sugar. At the same time tea became adopted as a necessary beverage for rich and poor alike, ousting the more expensive coffee and chocolate which had been popular in the second half of the seventeenth century. Tea, at first drunk in the Chinese manner, as a simple infusion of the tea leaves, with nothing added, came to be drunk, in the 1740s, with a little cream or milk, and sugar – so that by the nineteenth century these items were considered to be absolutely basic to even the poorest diet. The eating of cake, among the wealthy, went along with the ritual consumption of tea. As the hour of dinner, the main meal of the day, was pushed back from two or three o'clock in the afternoon at the start of the eighteenth century to six or seven at the end, 'afternoon tea' very nicely filled the gap. This meal, which started off as a light snack of cakes and biscuits washed down by tea, was enormously celebrated by the Victorians. It was in the nineteenth century that the tea table reached a glory unsurpassed. It must be remembered though that all the good things which we associate with the tea table were available only to the well-to-do. The mass of labouring poor in the nineteenth century could barely afford bread and cheese, let alone cakes. Perhaps occasionally, at fairs and at Christmas, they might indulge in 'fairings' – gingerbread, most likely, and plum pudding, if they were lucky. And towards the end of the century when conditions began slowly to improve and high tea became an established meal among the working and lower middle classes, especially in the North, cake might appear more regularly on the table.

I think however, that a tradition of baking must have continued more or less unbroken in the small farms of the North and West of Britain. In Wales and Scotland and Northern England, where the farmer's wife still cooked over an open fire, delicious varieties of oatcakes and 'flatbreads' cooked on griddles (scones, pancakes, crumpets, etc.) were made to centuries-old recipes. These were districts where peat turves were burnt, a fuel particularly suited to this kind of cooking. Pikelets, still popular in our family, originated in Wales as 'bara pyglyd' (pitchy bread), whence they spread to the Midlands. Emma Darwin told her daughter how, at the balls she used to go to in the 1820s, they used to be given white soup and pikelets for refreshments. 'It was a work of danger to eat slippery buttery pikelets in ball costume.' These leavened pancakes are similar to the better known crumpets and muffins beloved of the Victorians, but are made from a looser batter incorporating eggs. A recipe for 'Muffings' is given by Hannah Glasse in 1747. She explains why they must be toasted and torn apart, never cut, before being thickly spread with butter. In this way the honeycomb texture inside the muffin is retained, so that the butter has a chance to soak evenly through. To this end the two halves of the muffin are clapped together again and put to keep warm in front of the fire, being turned over and around once, so that the butter soaks into both halves.

The farmers of the North and West retained a greater degree of independence, and were comparatively less affected by the enclosures of the second half of the eighteenth century and the great agricultural depression of the first half of the nineteenth century which reduced the farm workers of the South, South West, Midlands and East Anglia to such poverty and misery. They had access to fuel which their southern compatriots lacked, and could therefore afford to bake in their own homes, instead of having to send food out to the local bakehouse. They were also more likely to keep a cow, chickens and a pig – and therefore to have available milk, cream, eggs and lard. From this may spring the reputation for excellent baking that Scotland and the northern counties now enjoy.

There is one cake however, so well known that dozens of recipes exist for it all over the country, which has rather a different history to the cakes in the spiced bread-dough tradition – and this is gingerbread. Medieval gingerbread was made from spiced breadcrumbs mixed to a paste with honey and coloured red with saunders (sandalwood) or alkanet (a root). The paste could be moulded, in elaborate wooden moulds, or rolled out and cut into shapes which would then be decorated, after drying in a cool oven, with gold leaf, gilded box leaves and gilt headed cloves, in heraldic designs (thus 'gilding the gingerbread'). The resulting confection, sold at fairs, and given as gifts must have tasted something like the Panforte still made in Siena today, and traditionally sold at their biennial medieval pageant — the Palio. A typical recipe, taken from Gervase Markham's *The English Housewife* (1615) specifies one quart of melted honey, ginger, pepper, liquorice, aniseeds and saunders, all ground and sieved, and added thereto with a quarter of a pint of claret or old ale, and enough white breadcrumbs to make a stiff paste. With the introduction of black treacle, however, in the seventeenth century, a by-product of sugar refining, gingerbread as we know it began to be made — at first, it is said, for Charles II. It soon replaced the medieval confection — the treacle proving a popular substitute for honey, as it imparted sweetness, flavour and colour all in one ingredient. Recipes for this type of gingerbread proliferated in the eighteenth century. It was particularly popular in the North, where it was often made with oatmeal — as in Yorkshire parkin.

The use of honey had been declining since the dissolution of the monasteries in the 1530s. Monks had been the country's foremost beekeepers, as much to provide wax for liturgical candles as honey. And as honey production waned, so sugar became cheaper and more widely available, until, by the eighteenth century, honey was used much as we use it now, as an additional luxury on the breakfast or tea table. The availability of sugar also led to a flowering in the art of sweet biscuit, pudding and pie manufacture. Biscuits, which started off in the Middle Ages as rusks of twice-cooked bread, similar to the modern French 'biscottes', were joined in the Tudor period by small cakes of sweetened and flavoured paste — twice cooked for longer keeping. Of this type of confection 'Shrewsbury cakes' are a typical example. Recipes for these, similar to the modern Shrewsbury biscuit, but lacking the currants, date back to the Tudors. Jumbles are also found in seventeenth-century cook books. At first used to describe any sweet confection joined together in knots, or twin rings (from the French 'gemmelle'), by the eighteenth century jumbles were always fatless wafers of sugar, flour and eggs, flavoured with rosewater, almonds or spices. By the eighteenth century quite a variety of biscuits and little cakes were being made, to accompany glasses of sweet wine, or dishes of tea, on lines familiar to us today.

Pastry and pies were of course well-known in the Middle Ages, but they were mostly of the savoury variety, or at least sweet and savoury mixed, as has survived in our mince pies. These were made in the seventeenth century, and doubtless in the fifteenth too, much as we make them today, but with the addition of shredded meat, preferably of Neat's tongue. Even Eliza Acton, in 1845, includes some 'fresh-boiled ox-tongue, or inside of roasted sirloin' in her own excellent recipe for mincemeat. It was in the eighteenth century that fruit pies and jam tarts became so popular and there are many good recipes for them — culminating in such deliciously rich confections as Bakewell Pudding (more commonly, and incorrectly, called a Tart), said to have been devised in the nineteenth century by the cook at the Rutland Arms in Bakewell, where it is still made.

As for the Englishman's pudding, this deserves a whole chapter to itself.

Originally, again, puddings were savoury concoctions — the term being applied to any chopped mixture of meats (often spiced and sweetened by the addition of currants and almonds) stuffed into the guts of an animal, and boiled. Later, the guts, being a nuisance to clean and prepare, were replaced by greased and floured cloths. By the end of the seventeenth century, the term pudding was beginning to be applied not only to sweet suet mixtures, boiled in a cloth, but to similar mixtures baked — and the English pudding had become a national speciality, eaten by rich and poor alike. It is interesting to note, however, that the English pudding *par excellence*, Christmas pudding, did not become associated with Christmas until the late eighteenth century. Earlier in the century, as plum pudding, it was eaten at Harvest suppers, its antecedents stretching back to the plum porridge, or pottage, of medieval and even earlier times — 'plum', of course, being used indiscriminately to describe dried fruits of all kinds. But by the 1690s, puddings in general were so well established that M. Misson, a French traveller in England, could write:

> They bake them (puddings) in an oven, they boil them with meat, they make them fifty several ways: BLESSED BE HE THAT INVENTED PUDDING, for it is a manna that hits the palates of all sorts of people; a manna, better than that of the wilderness, because the people are never weary of it. Ah, what an excellent thing is an English pudding! To come in pudding-time, is as much as to say, to come in the most lucky moment in the world. Give an Englishman a pudding, and he shall think it a noble treat in any part of the world.

SOURCES OF SUPPLY

Listings have been divided into sources of supply for the finished product, and a short list of mills specialising in the stronger and less familiar flours and grains we are beginning to use again in home baking. There are also two short sections dealing with other 'sweetmeats' — hand-made confectionery, and honeys, jams and preserves.

Puddings, Cakes, Biscuits and Shortbreads

SARAH NELSON, THE GINGERBREAD SHOP

Grasmere, Cumbria.
Sells (and will post) Grasmere Gingerbread, a traditional Cumbrian shortbread strongly flavoured with ginger.

OLD ORIGINAL BAKEWELL PUDDING SHOP

The Square, Bakewell, Derby.
Specialises in the original Bakewell Puddings (ancestor of the more familiar Bakewell Tart): personal shoppers only.

DICKINSON AND MORRIS LTD.

Melton Mowbray, Leicestershire LE13 1NW.
Makers of the Melton Hunt Cake, an extremely rich fruit cake, laced with Jamaican rum, originally produced (over 120 years ago) for the gentlemen, nobility and clergy of the Melton Hunt. Will dispatch the cakes to postal customers.

ASHBOURNE (DERBYSHIRE) GINGERBREAD SHOP

26 St. John Street, Ashbourne, Derby. Tel: Ashbourne (03355) 3227.
Makers of another regional delicacy of long standing – Ashbourne Gingerbread. Sold loose or in boxes, to personal shoppers only.

STRONGS

Market Place, Devizes, Wiltshire.
Bake, and sell (to personal shoppers only) Fermity, a pudding of corn, wheat, spices and sultanas.

ELISABETH THE CHEF LTD.

St. Marys Road, Leamington Spa, Warwickshire. Tel: (0926) 20731/5.
Supply a wide range of cakes by post: Majorcan Macaroon, a light fruit cake covered with macaroon, spinkled with almonds (also available as a Christmas macaroon, suitably decorated); rich Dundee; Brandy and Walnut Gateau (Easter only); Date and Brazil cake; Stollen, a fermented loaf cake made with butter, eggs, fruit, nuts and yeast; Oxford Cake; Birthday and Christmas cakes, in various sizes, iced and inscribed to order; Royal Warwick Cake; various shortbreads; Christmas pudding; Mandeltorte (Christmas only); Simnel cake (Easter only).

YOUNG AND SAUNDERS LTD.

5 Queensferry Street, Edinburgh EH2 4PD. Tel: (031) 225 6075.
Black Buns, Christmas puddings (1 lb., 2 lb. and 4 lb. weights). Rich Fruit Cake, Paradise Cake, Ginger Cake, Pineapple Cake, fruit cake with marzipan, shortbreads (Petticoat Tails, Shortbread fingers, Highlanders), Petit Fours, Artesse wafers, Ratafias, Crèpe Dentelles, Boudoir Fingers, Chocolate Olivers, Café Noir,

Brandy Snaps, Chamonix orange, Langue de Chat, Goustade hazelnut. All available to postal customers.

GRANTS OF CROYDON

High Street, Croydon. Tel: (01) 688 4400.
During the Crhtismas season only, will post the following: Christmas puddings (2 lb., 3½ lb. weights); Christmas cake; mince pies; Petit Fours.

HELIOS

Marlborough Mill, Macclesfield, Cheshire. Tel: (0625) 25460.
Mail order only. During Christmas season: Christmas cakes (2 lb., 3½ lb. weights); Plum pudding (2 lb.); Simnel cake; Irish Fruit cake; shortbread; Hanzana cake (all made by Ormeau bakers). Throughout the year: Rich English Fruit cake; Haig Fruit cake; Dry Sack raisin cake; Eccles Pie; Bakewell Pie; Mince Pie.

LANDMARK

Carrbridge, Inverness-shire, Scotland.
Mail order and personal shoppers. During the Christmas season only will post Whisky cake, Highlander shortbread, Petticoat Tails and shortbread fingers.

KEYLINK LTD.

Link House, Papermill Road, Sheffield S5 0EA.
Mail order only. Will mail Tasmanian Cherry and Sultana cake, and a rich Dark Fruit cake with rum and brandy flavouring.

GRAYS OF WORCESTER LTD.

Orchard Street, Worcester WR5 3DP. Tel: Worcester (0905) 352388.
Black Bun (or Twelfth Cake), Dundee Cakes (ready iced), Mr. Guinness Cake, Mince Pies, shortbread, Christmas puddings. Mail order, throughout the year.

MATTHES BAKERIES

Great Yarmouth, Norfolk.
Mail order, Christmas season only: Norfolk Fruit cakes, Christmas puddings.

S. MOORES

Morecombelake, Bridport, Devon.
Dorset knot biscuits, shortbread and Easter cakes. Personal shoppers only.

FORTNUM AND MASON

Piccadilly, London W1A 1ER.
Shortbread, fruit cake, Dundee cake and a wide variety of traditional biscuits available by mail order and to personal shoppers.

Flours, etc.

S. MAYALL AND SON

Lea Hall, Harmer Hill, Shrewsbury. Tel: Bomere Heath 342.
Compost grown stoneground flours and cereals; wholewheat flour, rye flour, 85 per cent extraction flour, barley flour, oatmeal and oatmeal flakes (brand name Pimhill) can all be bought direct from the mill in bulk (for collection), for delivery within a small local radius or by post. Write to the mill for details. They can also advise you if the flours are available through any retail outlets in your particular area.

BUYBULK LTD.

Tunnel Bank Road, Bourne, Lincs. Tel: Bourne 3291.
A range of flours for home-baking available in bulk either by mail order or for collection from Buybulk itself: Whitworths Plain and Self-Raising; Golden Grain Wheatmeal; Supers Flour (specifically for bread); Allinson's Wholewheat Plain and Farmhouse Self-Raising, both stoneground; Allinson's Farmhouse Plain; Granary Meal.

YOUNG AND SAUNDERS LTD.

5 Queensferry Street, Edinburgh EH2 4PD. Tel: (031) 225 6075.
Irish Plain flour, Soda Bread flour and Cake flour, all available by mail order and to personal shoppers.

INFINITY FOODS

25 North Street, Brighton. Tel: Brighton 63563.
A fascinating shop, and although they can supply goods by mail order, it is worth paying them a visit just to see the extraordinary range of foods available. They can supply the following flours and cereals by mail order, and in bulk and smaller quantities to personal shoppers: stoneground 100 per cent English Wholewheat flour; stoneground 85 per cent English wheat; rye flour; barley flour; whole rice flour; fine cornmeal; coarse cornmeal; maize meal; soya flour; buckwheat flour; oatmeal (fine, medium and coarse) and wheat bran. They can also supply a range of whole grain cereals: pot barley; whole oat groats; roasted

and unroasted buck wheat; millet; bulgar and couscous.

W. BROWN LTD.

Lodge Lane, Derby. Tel: 0332 45232.
Mills a wide variety of stoneground flours: 100 per cent flour, barley, rye, rice, maize, soya and millet. All can be purchased from the mill itself, in any quantities. Deliveries are made twice weekly, and sometimes more frequently, in the London area (for larger quantities only, so that it might be worth thinking about a co-operative order with a number of friends) and regular deliveries can be made in the immediate Derby area.

N. R. STOATE AND SONS LTD.

Cann Mills, Shaftesbury, Dorset.
Flours milled from locally grown, untreated wheat. Write to the mill for details of availability.

CULPEPER

59 Ebury Street, London SW1W 0NZ.
100 per cent wholewheat flour sold in three pound bags to personal shoppers and mail order customers.

Confectionery

The following suppliers, listed alphabetically, specialise in hand-made confectionery and with one exception will all supply mail order customers.

BONNET AND SONS

Huntriss Row, Scarborough.
Supply their own hand-made chocolates to mail order customers.

CHARBONNEL ET WALKER

31 Old Bond Street, London W1. Tel: 01 629 4396.
Wide range of hand-made chocolates and other confectionery, available to personal shoppers and mail order customers.

DANFOOD LTD.

Box 21, Bishops Stortford, Herts.
Selection of Danish chocolates, produced by Anthon Berg, available to mail order customers only.

GRAYS OF WORCESTER LTD.

Orchard Street, Worcester WR5 3DP. Tel: 0905 352388.
After dinner Mints, choclate liqueur prunes, plain and milk chocolate truffles, hand-made Belgian chocolates, Old English fudge, sugared almonds and Turkish Delight available to mail order customers only.

FORTNUM AND MASON

Piccadilly, London W1A 1ER. Tel: 01 734 8040.
Will send their own sugared almonds, liqueur chocolates, slimline peppermints, the Fortnum and Mason standard assortment of hand-made plain chocolates, almond Butter Crunch and Griottes en Cognac to customers throughout the UK.

HELIOS

Marlborough Mill, Macclesfield, Cheshire. Tel: 0625 25460.
Delice's confectionery, manufactured by the Belgian firm Corne Toison d'Or, mainly by hand. Two selections – Blue Ribbon and Gold Ribbon – available to mail order customers.

INTERCHOC LTD.

Key House, Horton Road, West Drayton, Middlesex. Tel: West Drayton 49202.
Supply boxes of hand-made English chocolates to mail order customers only.

KEYLINK LTD.

Link House, Papermill Road, Sheffield S5 0EA. Tel: 07415 2088.
Also sell the Delice range (see Helios above) to mail order customers only. Also available: Mondose chocolate liqueurs, Swiss chocolates in a range of flavours imported from the Swiss firms Perrier-Villars and Maestrani, marzipan sweets from Schluckwerder, Weseke dragees, marrons glacés and Montelimar Nougat from Nougats Vieille France in Velars.

PRESTAT

24 South Molton Street, London W1. Tel: 01 629 4838.
Hand-made chocolates and truffles available to personal shoppers only.

ROBERT JACKSON

171-2 Piccadilly, London W1. Tel: 01 493 1033.
Jackson's own 'confiseur' produces a range of hand-made chocolates (thirty different flavours in all) plus Jacksons Vienna Mints, fresh cream truffles (rum

and plain), marzipan fruits, cherries in brandy, fruits in liqueur and liqueur chocolates. All available to personal shoppers and by post from the Piccadilly shop.

WHITTARDS AND CO. LTD.

111 Fulham Road, London SW3. Tel: 01 589 4261.
Bendicks chocolates (Bittermints, chocolate crème de menthe, Superfine Assorted and Mint Crisps) and Turkish Delight (Rahat Lacoum, Rahat Lacoum with almonds, crème de menthe) all available by post and from the shop itself.

YOUNG AND SAUNDERS LTD.

5 Queensferry Street, Edinburgh EH2 4PD. Tel: 031 225 6075.
Hand-made chocolates (made for Young and Saunders by Charbonnel et Walker) available to mail order customers and personal shoppers in a variety of flavours and types.

Honey, Jams and Preserves

DANFOOD LTD.

Box 21, Bishops Stortford, Herts.
A range of Danish preserves — cherry, cranberry, blackcurrant, redcurrant, rowan and apple — available to mail order customers only.

FORTNUM AND MASON

Piccadilly, London W1A 1ER. Tel: 01 734 8040.
Sell (and will send to mail order customers) a wide range of preserves, 'exotic' honeys, honeycomb and pure English flower honey.

L. GARVIN AND CO. LTD.

Garvin House, 158 Twickenham Road, Isleworth, Middlesex TW7 7DL.
Tel: 01 560 7171.
Mail order service available for a variety of honeys (write to them for a complete list, as availability varies), in 7 lb., 14 lb. and 56 lb. packs.

GRAYS OF WORCESTER LTD.

Orchard Street, Worcester WR5 3DP. Tel: 0905 352388.
A range of preserves — peach with Benedictine, apricot with almonds, strawberry with Curacao, damson with Kummel, cherry with almonds and brandy, and

Swiss black cherry – sold in a special pack. A marmalade 'pack' is also available, containing orange marmalades variously flavoured with brandy, rum, whisky, Drambuie and Cointreau, together with an orange ginger marmalade.

HOLGATES HONEY FARM LTD.

Cadwgan Place, Aberdaeron, Cardiganshire. Tel: Aberdaeron 445.
Produce a range of honeys and marmalades, made from traditional recipes. Write to them for further information on availability.

THE HORSELESS CARRIAGE

Warkworth, Morpeth, Northumberland. Tel: Warkworth 444.
A range of honeys and traditional marmalades. Write to them for full details.

INFINITY FOODS

25 North Road, Brighton, Sussex. Tel: Brighton 63563.
A wide variety of honey available, which they will post if necessary to mail order customers, although they prefer to sell to personal shoppers. Write to them for further details of particular honeys, as supplies vary from time to time.

DIA AND MARION JONES

Bryn, Fourcrosses, Pwllheli, Caernarvonshire.
Produce 'Welsh Lady' apricot and brandy preserves. Write to them for further details.

JUSTIN DE BLANK PROVISIONS LTD.

42 Elizabeth Street, London SW1 9NZ. Tel: 01 730 0605.
Home-made jams and marmalades available to personal shoppers only – although they will occasionally post items to customers unable to reach the shop, so it is worth enquiring. The following marmalades are available: four fruit, bitter lemon, grapefruit, seville orange, and dark amber. Also stock Mrs. Whitehouse's raspberry jam, strawberry conserve, London honey, heather honey-combs, Miel du Mont-Ventoux (lavender flower honey), Devon heather honey, Polish pinewood honey and clear or set clover honey.

LANDMARK

Carrbridge, Inverness-shire, Scotland.
Will post to mail order customers Broomfield Scottish heather honey in 1 lb. jars.

YOUNG AND SAUNDERS LTD.

5 Queensferry Street, Edinburgh EH2 4PD. Tel: 031 225 6075.
A wide range of marmalades, including Isle of Arran and whisky marmalades, and a selection from the Elsenham and Tiptree ranges. Also Tiptree and Hero preserves, and a range of honeys: Strathmore liqueur, orange blossom, acacia, Hymettus, wild flower, Canadian clover, Honduras, lime blossom, rosemary, Tasmanian, cut comb, honey and malt, French ling heather. All available to mail order customers and personal shoppers.

Wild honey can be ordered in quarter hundredweights direct from the following suppliers:

J. I. Rodale and Co. Ltd., Berkhamstead, Hertfordshire.

The Organic Food Service, Churston Ferrers, South Devon.

Ranolan Health Foods Ltd., Walgrave-on-Thames, Berkshire.

Allinson Ltd., 210-214 Cambridge Heath Road, London E2.

Beer, Malt Whisky and English Wines

BEER: REAL ALE

Michael Hardman

Britain's vineyards don't cover the slopes of breathtaking hills; nor are Britain's chateaux to be found tucked away in the valleys of romantic rivers. The British vines don't bear grapes, but hops, and find their roots in the rolling countryside of Kent and Worcestershire; the chateaux, which mix the hops with the barley to make beer, crop up among the steelworks of Sheffield, the clatter of the Cardiff docks and the bleakness of the Black Country.

The contrast between the way the French and the British go about producing their national drinks is not only enormous – it is downright disturbing. And so is the comparison between the attitudes of drinkers in the two countries.

Whereas the French wine industry is geared to variety, with each region jealously guarding the identity of its local *appelation*, with more than a little help from the law, and a national, nay international, scandal blowing up when someone tries to push foreign wine into the country's glasses, the British have of late been letting themselves be robbed of their local individuality in choice of beer and have in many cases been led to prefer alien brews.

Big business has been the main culprit in the rape of Britain's beer tradition. A series of mergers and takeovers in the late 1950s and throughout the 1960s led inevitably to the closure of hundreds of local breweries. The pubs they had served for centuries were suddenly told to sell a strange brew. The customers grumbled for a week or two and then showed the white flag. Gone were names which people had associated with their nights out since their eighteenth birthday, and often earlier. Almonds of Standish, Harmans of Uxbridge, Evan Evans Bevan of the Vale of Neath, Flowers of Stratford, Campbell, Hope and King of Edinburgh . . . the list of derelict chateaux goes on for pages. Almost everyone over the age of twenty-five will have known (and perhaps loved) at least one of the hundreds of brews that died as a result of the brewers' frantic rationalisation policies of the 1960s.

As if the closure of breweries and the consequent disappearance of choice were not enough, the brewers got it into their heads at about the same time to alter the very taste of our beer by introducing methods of processing, packaging and dispensing which had been lying around latent for many years. These new methods involved taking all the character out of the beer by filtering it and pasteurising it before it left the brewery; then packaging it in contraptions which didn't allow it to gain flavour like the traditional barrel had; and finally forcing it from cellar to bar by an injection of gas instead of drawing it by a manual pump or letting it flow straight from the cask.

These innovations resulted in two new kinds of beer: keg, which was hailed as the beer-drinker's Messiah; and top-pressure beer, which had many of the advantages that keg had to the brewer and licensee and many of the disadvantages for the drinker. Keg beer was, and still is, subjected to every process imaginable: it is filtered, nearly always pasteurised, invariably pressurised like an aerosol; it tastes bland and gassy. Top-pressure beer, which is incorrectly described as draught beer by many brewers, is stored in barrels like the beer of old and often reaches the pub in its natural condition, but it is then connected to a gas cylinder and blown up to the bar just like keg beer.

The brewers say that these new processes were brought in because draught beer was prone to go off quickly if it wasn't treated with loving care. The new beers, they say, are a positive benefit to the drinker because they are much more consistent.

It would be foolish to say that the brewers were entirely wrong. There was — and always will be — a lot of bad beer around, beer which is ruined by landlords who haven't the necessary skills or patience to keep it in its peak condition. Pressurisation does at least make it more difficult for beer to go off, but it must be regarded as an easy way out: a short cut in the search for ways to improve the quality of the beer. The brewers will also say, with some justification, that many people prefer the blander, fizzier beers which have been introduced over the past fifteen years or so — and they can point to the remarkable success of lager as evidence of their claim.

What the brewers have in the main failed to grasp, however, is that not everyone likes — or can even stomach — these strange brews. They want character in their pint and will shun consistency if that means consistent mediocrity.

Only about a third of Britain's seventy-odd thousand pubs still sell beer which has not been subjected to unnatural processes. The rest serve nothing but keg or top-pressure beer. It is this situation which led to the formation in 1971 of CAMRA, the Campaign for Real Ale, which pledged itself from the outset to fight for a better deal for those drinkers who wanted, but in many areas couldn't get, beer brewed and served in the traditional manner.

CAMRA's main platform is to protect choice for the drinker. The organisation has no secret rules which force its members never to drink processed beer, nor does it deny people who like these beers the right to drink them. Most of the 25,000 or so pubs which sell the real thing do, in fact, also offer pressurised products and CAMRA is more than pleased to see this state of affairs continuing.

CAMRA was founded by four young men from the North of England who had experienced the death of the British chateaux at first hand. The organisation grew slowly at first, with membership restricted to a few dozen friends of the founders in Lancashire and Cheshire. A year after the Campaign's formation, the founders called an annual meeting in Nuneaton, Warwickshire, and invited many of their friends who were living in various corners of the country. CAMRA was successfully launched on a national basis at that meeting in the spring of 1972 and since then it has never looked back. The membership rose to 1,400 by 1973 and to 10,000 in 1974. Now it stands at 30,000 – and the Campaign is run on a local level by more than 100 well-organised branches.

CAMRA's actual successes, like its membership, were slow in coming. But a number of breweries have identified themselves with the Campaign by actively promoting their traditional products instead of going all out to force pressurised beer down the throats of unsuspecting drinkers. These companies include Thwaites of Blackburn, who have 400 pubs in the North West, Wadworths of Devizes, who have 120 houses in the West, and Shepherd Neame of Faversham, who have 210 houses in the South East. These brewers were already selling traditional beer in the majority of their pubs, but CAMRA has also succeeded in persuading brewers who were serving little or no unpressurised beer to switch on to the real thing.

Paines of St. Neots, for instance, who were described by CAMRA a year ago as 'a complete waste of time', are now offering traditional ale in 11 of their 24 pubs; Arkells of Swindon have made a major policy reversal in turning off the gas in many of their 67 houses; Fullers of London are weighing up the pros and cons of switching back to unpressurised beer in their 116 pubs.

Even the big brewers are beginning to take notice.

The six major brewing companies in Britain own two-thirds of our pubs and produce three-quarters of our beer. They are the ones who are mostly to blame for the demise of British beer. Now, however, two of them – Watney Mann and Courage – have begun experiments to see if there is a demand for real beer.

Watneys have eight breweries in Britain and only three of them – in Manchester, Halifax and Trowbridge – produce real beer. But they have recently decided to test market unpressurised ale in the South East, one of the beer deserts they helped to create. Courage, who have eight breweries, all but two of them producing *some* real beer, are turning off the gas in sixty pubs in London and the Home Counties to test the reaction of their customers.

Much of this activity within the breweries has resulted from the interest generated by the *Good Beer Guide*, an annual publication compiled by CAMRA and available to the public through the bookshops. The first guide, issued last year, listed 1,600 pubs in England, Wales and the Isle of Man where the best of real beer could be found. This year's guide, which is almost twice as big, lists 2,700 pubs and covers Scotland for the first time. All 30,000 copies printed sold out in a month and the demand shows no sign of letting up.

The *Good Beer Guide* is, fortunately, one indication that the rape of the British chateaux might have ended. A new era could be dawning for British beer.

SOURCES OF SUPPLY: THE INDEPENDENT BREWERS

Listed below are most of the main independent brewers. We have included the names of the various draught beers they produce, and, where possible, the names and addresses of one or two pubs where the beer can be enjoyed. For more detailed information, the reader is referred to the CAMRA Guide mentioned in the introduction.

ADNAMS AND CO. LTD.

Sole Bay Brewery, East Green, Southwold, Suffolk.
Adnams produce two varieties of old ale, or winter brew – Strong Ale and a draught barley wine called Tally Ho – and a distinctive Mild. Most of the 71 tied houses are in East Suffolk. A full list of their names and addresses can be obtained from the brewery.

J. ARKELL AND SONS LTD.

Kingsdown Brewery, Upper Stratton, Swindon, Wilts SN2 6RV.
Most of the tied houses serving Arkells beer are within a five-mile radius of Swindon, but not all of them serve the two draught bitters brewed (Bitter and Best Bitter Beer) unpressurised. Try The Bear, Charnham Street, Hungerford, Bucks.; The Bakers Arms, Badbury, Wilts., or the Borough Arms, High Street, Wootten Bassett, Wilts.

THE WOLVERHAMPTON AND DUDLEY BREWERIES LTD. (BANKS)

Park Brewery, Wolverhampton WV1 4NY.
The brewery brews both Banks and Hansons beers (draught Mild and a Bitter) both of which are properly served in most of the 800 tied houses.

GEORGE BATEMAN AND SONS LTD.

Salem Bridge Brewery, Wainfleet, Skegness, Lincolnshire.
More than 100 tied houses within a forty-mile radius of Wainfleet serve Bateman's 'Good Honest Ales', Bitter and Light Mild, untainted by pressure.

DANIEL BATHAM AND SONS LTD.

Delph Brewery, Brierley Hill, West Midlands.
Highly prized strong beers (a Bitter and two Milds, one light, one strong dark) available in only eight tied houses. Try The Vine, Delph Road, The Delph, Brierley Hill – right next door to the brewery itself, and well worth a visit.

BELHAVEN BREWERY CO. LTD.

Dunbar, East Lothian EH42 1PE.
CAMRA rates Belhaven Beers (Export, Heavy and Light draught bitters) as possibly the best in Scotland. The brewery can supply a full list of their forty tied houses on request. For starters, try The Royal Oak, 169 Stirling Street, Denny; The Old Abbey Tavern, Kirkgate, Dunfermline (Fife); The Dutch Mill, 7 Queens Road, Aberdeen (Grampian); J. B. Bennet's Bar, 8 Leven Street, Edinburgh; The Firhill Tavern, 740 Garscube Road, Glasgow; or the Bowbridge Bar, 1 Mains Road, Dundee.

BODDINGTON'S BREWERIES LTD.

Strangeways Brewery, Manchester M60 31EL.
Brews Bitter, Mild and Best Mild, the Bitter being, by repute, one of the strongest in Britain. The brewery will supply lists of their 280 tied houses on request. Worth remembering that not one of the 280 serve the beer under pressure.

BORDER BREWERIES (WREXHAM) LTD.

Wrexham, Clwya.
Two hundred houses, many of which serve the beers – Bitter, Light, Medium and Strong Dark Mild – unpressurised.

S. A. BRAIN AND CO. LTD.

The Old Brewery, St. Mary Street, Cardiff.
Most of the 100 or so tied houses (nearly all of them in the Cardiff and Swansea areas) serve the Draught Bitter, SA Best Draught Bitter and Red Dragon Draught Dark by traditional methods.

W. H. BRAKSPEAR AND SONS LTD.

The Brewery, Henley on Thames, Oxfordshire.
Brews Pale Ale, Special Bitter Ale, XXX Mild and XXXX (stronger and darker and only available in a few pubs all the year round). Write to the brewery for a list of their tied houses. There are 130 in all, including some considered to be the most attractive pubs in Britain. Try the Belgian Arms, Holyport Green, Holyport, Berks., as a foretaste of other delights.

MATTHEW BROWN AND CO. LTD.

Lion Brewery, Blackburn, Lancs.
Brew a draught Bitter and a Mild, but served correctly in only a very few of the 600 tied houses in Lancashire and Cumberland.

BUCKLEYS BREWERY LTD.

The Brewery, Gilbert Road, Llanelli, Dyfed.
Most of the 180 tied houses serve the beer (Standard Bitter, Best Bitter and Mild) unpressurised.

BURTONWOOD BREWERY CO. (FORSHAWS) LTD.

Bold Lane, Burtonwood, Warrington.
Well liked beers, Bitter and Mild, served correctly in most of the 300 tied houses in the north-west and North Wales.

J. W. CAMERON AND CO. LTD.

Green Bank Offices, Lion Brewery, Hartlepool, Co. Durham.
Of the Best Bitter, dark Mild and Strongarm Ale brewed by Camerons, the Strongarm enjoys a considerable reputation amongst the *cognoscenti*. Cameron Beers are one of the few real ales readily available in Durham, Yorkshire and the north-east.

CASTLETOWN BREWERY LTD.

Victoria Road, Castletown, Isle of Man.
The Pure Beer Act, a Manx law which has been in force since 1874, forbids the use of any ingredients other than malt hops and sugar in brewing the island beers. So the chances of finding anything but real ale on the island are virtually nil. Write to Castletown for a list of their forty tied houses scattered round the island.

W. M. DARLEY LTD.

The Brewery, Thorne, Doncaster, South Yorkshire.
Over 100 tied houses, most of which serve Darleys IPA (India Pale Ale) and Darleys Dark by traditional methods.

DAVENPORTS BREWERY LTD.

The Brewery, Bath Row, Birmingham 15 1NB.
Davenports operate a rather unusual home delivery service, in addition to supplying their 112 tied houses. The pubs are spread over a wide area – Birmingham, Coventry, Leamington, Rugby and Warwick all have Davenport pubs. Further afield, Davenport tied houses can be found in Oxfordshire, Shropshire and Worcestershire, with a few outposts in Bristol and South Wales.

DONNINGTON BREWERY

Stow-on-the-Wold, Gloucestershire GL54 1EP.
Privately owned by L. C. Arkel. The two Bitters (BB and SBA) are served unpressurised in some, but not all, of the seventeen tied houses. Try The Coach and Horses, Ganborough, Glos., and The Queens Head, Stow-on-the-Wold, Glos.

ELDRIDGE POPE AND CO.

The Dorchester Brewery, Dorchester, Dorset.
Brews Best Bitter and a stronger, special IPA, XXXX (a stronger, dark ale sometimes available in winter) and a Double Mild. Only a few of the 200 tied houses serve the beers unpressurised. Try The Three Horseshoes, Askerswell, Dorset; The New London Tavern, Poole, Dorset; and The Rose and Crown, Trent, Dorset.

ELGOOD AND SONS LTD.

North Brink Brewery, Wisbech, Cambridgeshire.
Highly regarded draught Bitter and Mild, but served unpressurised in only a few of the 200 or so tied houses. Try The Red Lion, 15 High Street, March, Cam.; The Blue Bell, Peterborough, Cam.; The Boat in Whittlesey; and The Angel or The Kings Head in Wisbech itself.

FULLER, SMITH AND TURNER LTD.

The Griffin Brewery, Chiswick, London W4 2QB.
One of a vanishing breed – the London Brewer. Ten tied houses sell draught ale, most of them in the London area. Fullers Extra Special Bitter, the strongest of the three bitters they brew, is reputedly the strongest known draught beer in the country. Try The Star Tavern, 6 Belgrave Mews West, London SW1; The Dove, 19 Upper Mall, London W6; The White Hart, 70 High Street, Hampton; The Prince Albert, 30 Hampton Road, Twickenham. Fullers will supply a full list of all their tied houses on request.

GEORGE GALE AND CO. LTD.

The Brewery, Horndean, Portsmouth, Hampshire PO8 0DA.
Horndean Special Bitter, Bitter, Light Mild, Dark Mild and XXXXX, a winter brewed ale. Served without pressure in all but two of the 89 tied houses.

GREENE KING (BURY)

Westgate Brewery, Bury St. Edmunds, Suffolk.
The draught beers have a good reputation, but they are getting difficult to find

'uncontaminated' by pressure. The IPA Ale, IA Light Bitter, Light Mild, XX Mild and Abbot Ale should be found unpressurised at the following pubs: The Nutshell (one of several pubs claiming to be the smallest in Britain) in Bury St. Edmunds; The Rising Sun (also in Bury); The Fox, Great Bradley, Suffolk.

HALL AND WOODHOUSE

The Brewery, Blandford Forum, Dorset.
Increasingly difficult to find their beers unpressurised, but when tracked down (mainly in Dorset, West Hampshire and parts of Somerset and Wiltshire) the Bitter, Best Bitter and Mild are well worth sampling. Try The Halsey Arms, Pulham, Dorset.

HARDY'S AND HANSONS LTD.

Kimberley Brewery, Nottingham NG16 2NS.
A prizewinning Best Bitter, properly served in most of the tied houses in and around Nottingham, Derby and Chesterfield, where draught Mild is also available. Visit The Crown, Middle Street, Beeston, Notts.; and The Miners Arms, Inkermann Lane, Selston, Notts.

HARTLEY'S (ULVERSTON) LTD.

The Old Brewery, Ulverston, Cumbria.
Two Bitters brewed, of which the XB is the more highly regarded. Both properly dispensed in all of the tied houses throughout the Lake District and the Furness Peninsula. Try The Waggon and Horses, 27 St. Georges Quay, Lancaster; The New Inn, Yealand Road, Yealand Conyers; The New Hill, Robinson Place, Bowness-on-Windermere; or The Railway in Ulverston.

HARVEY AND SONS

Bridge Wharf Brewery, Lewes, East Sussex.
Bitter, Best Bitter, Mild, XXXX (old), and Elizabethan Ale on draught – but in only a few of the tied houses, most of which are in East Sussex. Try The Merrydown Wine Bar, New Road, Brighton; The Bell, High Street, Burwash; The New Inn, Hadlow Down; and The Black Horse, Rottingdean, Sussex.

HIGSONS BREWERY LTD.

Stanhope Street, Liverpool L8 5RE.
Draught Bitter and Mild usually dispensed by hand pumps in most of the tied houses in and around Merseyside. Visit The Wheatsheaf, 186 East Prescot Road, Liverpool; The Globe, Cases Street, Liverpool City Centre; The Brewery Tap,

Grapes, 67 Stanhope Street, Liverpool 8.

HOLDENS BREWERY LTD.

Hopden Brewery, George Street, Woodsetton, Dudley, West Midlands.
Only a very few tied houses (try The Park, George Street, Wood Setton) but most of them serve draught Mild. An old ale is brewed only at Christmas, and can occasionally be tracked down. Write to the brewery for a full list of their tied houses.

JOSEPH HOLT LTD.

Derby Brewery, Empire Street, Cheetham, Manchester M3 1JD.
Good Bitter and Mild, correctly dispensed in all of the 80 tied houses in and around Manchester. Try The Griffin, Didsbury Road, Heaton Mersey, Stockport; and The Junction, Station Road, Cheadle Hulme.

HOME BREWERY CO. LTD.

The Brewery, Mansfield Road, Daybrook, Nottinghamshire.
Over 400 tied houses, most within a fifty-mile radius of Nottingham City Centre. The draught Bitter and Mild is usually served by traditional methods. Try The Barley Mow, Basford Road, Nottingham.

HOOK NORTON BREWERY CO. LTD.

Hook Norton, nr. Banbury, Oxfordshire.
Draught Bitter and Mild ('hookey') dispensed by manual pumps in 33 of the 34 tied houses in and around Hook Norton. Try The Butchers Arms, Balscote; The Old Reindeer, Banbury; The Crown and Tuns, Deddington; The Faulkland Arms, Great Tew; The Turf Tavern, St. Helens Passage, New College Lane (which is the only Hook Norton pub in Oxford, and therefore worth a visit).

T. HOSKINS LTD.

Beaumanor Road, Leicester.
Only one tied house: The Red Lion, Park Street, Market Bosworth, which is generally considered to be excellent. The draught Bitter and Mild can be bought from the off-licence adjoining the brewery in Beaumont Road. Take empty bottles, jugs or buckets.

HYDES ANVIL BREWERY LTD.

46 Moss Lane West, Manchester M15 5PH.
All fifty of the tied houses, in the Manchester area for the most part, dispense

draught Bitter, Mild and Best Bitter unpressurised. Try The Old Plough, Green Lane, Ashton-on-Mersey; The Red Lion, Stockport Road, Denton; The Gateway, Wilmslow Road, Didsbury; and The Grand Junction, Chichester Road, Hulme.

JENNINGS BROTHERS LTD.

The Castle Brewery, Cockermouth, Cumbria.
Seventy-nine out of the eighty tied houses in the Lake District serve the distinctive draught Mild and Bitter from manual bar pumps. Two in particular are worth visiting: The Ghyll Yeat, Blindcrake, Cumbria; and The Wheatsheaf, Cockermouth Road, Embleton. In both, the beer is fetched from the cellar by hand.

KING AND BARNES LTD.

18 Bishopric, Horsham, West Sussex.
Highly regarded, the draught ales are traditionally dispensed in most of the tied houses in and around Horsham. Look out for the 'old' ale, brewed in winter. You should be able to find it at The Stag, Balls Cross; The Cherry Tree, Copthorne; and The Kings Arms, Horsham.

J. W. LEES AND CO. LTD.

Greengate Brewery, Middleton, Manchester M24 2AX.
Bitter, Best Mild and Mild. The Bitter in particular is one of the strongest draught beers in the north-west. Nearly two hundred tied houses in Lancashire, Cheshire and North Wales serve the beers without pressure. Try The Travellers Call, Stockport Road, Bradbury; The Prince of Wales, The Green Gartley; The Grand Junction, Chichester Road, Hulme; and The Puckersley, 22 Narrowgate Brow, Royton.

MACLAY AND CO. LTD.

Thistle Brewery, Alloa, Clackmannanshire, Scotland.
Draught Maclays Export, SPA and Pale Ale can be found in 12 of the 26 tied houses in Clackmannanshire, Ayrshire and Lanarkshire. Worth drinking.

MARSTON, THOMPSON AND EVERSHED LTD.

Shonall Road, Burton-on-Trent DE14 2BW.
Over 500 tied houses from Hampshire to Cumbria serve draught BB, Pedigree and a draught Mild – all three beers excellent. Try The Beehive, Honeywall, Penkhull, Stoke-on-Trent; and The Albion, Shobnall Road, Burton-on-Trent.

MITCHELLS OF LANCASTER (BREWERS) LTD.

11 Moor Lane, Lancaster.
Fifty tied houses, all within a ten-mile radius of Lancaster, dispense the excellent Bitter, Extra Special Bitter and a dark Mild by the traditional methods.

MORRELLS BREWERY LTD.

The Lion Brewery, St. Thomas Street, Oxford.
A few of the 140 tied houses serve the Bitter and Light Ale (and occasionally the stronger College Ale) without pressure. Try The Rose and Crown, Launton, Blackthorn.

OKELL AND SON LTD.

Falcon Brewery, Douglas, Isle of Man.
All of the Okell tied houses on the island dispense the draught Mild and Bitter by traditional methods.

J. C. AND R. H. PALMER

Old Brewery, West Bay Road, Bridport, Dorset.
Try the Eight Bells, Church Street, Beauminster; The George, Bothenhampton; and The Kings Arms, North Akington, Bridport for draught Best Bitter and Mild. Most of the other Palmer tied houses serve the beer under pressure, ruining what is generally considered to be a fine ale.

T. D. RIDLEY AND SONS LTD.

Hartford End, Chelmsford, Essex.
Highly acclaimed beers, served by traditional methods in all of the 60 or so tied houses in central and north-west Essex.

FREDERIC ROBINSON LTD.

Unicorn Brewery, Stockport, Cheshire.
Most of the 300 tied houses (in north-east Cheshire, Derbyshire, and North Wales) serve the Robinson draught Best Bitter and Best Mild in the approved manner.

G. RUDDLE AND CO. LTD.

The Brewery, Langham, Oakham, Rutland (Leics.).
Extremely popular beers, including a Bitter, County Ale (exceptionally strong) and a draught Barley Wine, available only in the winter. Not all of the Ruddles

tied houses serve unpressurised beer. Try The Crown, Uppingham, Leics.; The Fox and Goose, Illiston on the Hill, Leics.; and The Kings Arms, Wing, Leics.

SELBY BREWERY LTD.

The Brewery, Millgate, Selby, North Yorkshire.
An unusual and very distinctive real ale, available only at the Board, Market Place, Howden, Yorkshire. There are one or two other free trade outlets – call or write to the brewery for details.

SHEPHERD NEAME LTD.

Faversham Brewery, 17 Court Street, Faversham, Kent ME13 2AX.
Distinctive beers – Best Bitter, Light Mild (very hard to find, but worth searching for), Mild and Old English Stock Ale, a strong draught easier to locate in winter. True draught dispensing in most of the tied houses in East Kent, Sussex and a few of the Greater London pubs.

JAMES SHIPSTONE AND SONS LTD.

Star Brewery, New Basford, Nottingham.
Two hundred and fifty tied houses in Nottingham, Leicester, Derbyshire and dotted around Lincolnshire and Yorkshire, all dispensing draught Bitter and Mild by traditional methods.

JPS BREWERIES LTD.

Dennis Brewery, Brettell Lane, Brierley Hill, West Midlands.
Best Bitter, Mild and a strong dark winter brew, Old Ale (from October to March only) served unpressurised in the breweries' sixteen tied houses.

SAMUEL SMITH OLD BREWERY

The Old Brewery, Tadcaster, North Yorkshire.
Bitter, Light Mild, 4X Best Mild and Strong Ale traditionally dispensed in most of the three hundred tied houses in the north-west.

TIMOTHY TAYLOR AND CO. LTD.

Knowle Spring Brewery, Keighley, Yorkshire.
Nearly thirty tied houses, a good many of them in Keighley, and every one of them dispensing a range of excellent ales in the approved manner – Best Bitter, Golden Best Light Mild available in all of the houses, Draught Landlord only available at The Hare and Hounds, Lane Ends Lane, Chisley, Old Town, Hebden Bridge, Yorkshire.

THEAKSTON (MASHAM) LTD.

Wellgarth, Masham, Ripon, Yorks.
Best Bitter and Theakston's Old Peculiar (one of the strongest in the country) on draught in all of the sixteen tied houses. Try and visit The Holly Hill, Richmond, North Yorkshire or The White Bear, next door to the brewery itself, in Masham.

DANIEL THWAITES AND CO. LTD.

Star Brewery, Blackburn, Lancashire NN1 5BU.
Nearly 400 tied houses, a good many of them concentrated in the north-east, from the Lake District down through Lancashire to Cheshire, although there are a good many of them beyond this particular pale. All dispensing draught Bitter, Mild and Best Mild in the traditional manner. Try to visit The Kings Head, King Street, Blackburn, which CAMRA considers a fine example of the traditional Lancastrian alehouse.

WADWORTH AND CO. LTD.

Northgate Brewery, Devizes, Wiltshire SN10 1JW.
Pale Ale, India Pale Ale, 6X, Old Timer (very strong, and only available on draught during the winter months) and Mild Ale available, and highly thought of, in nearly all of the 160 tied houses in and near Wiltshire. Write to the Brewery for a full list.

S. H. WARD AND CO. LTD.

Sheaf Brewery, Ecclesham Road, Sheffield, Yorkshire.
More than 100 tied houses, most of them in or around Sheffield, all serving draught Bitter, Best Bitter and Mild Ale in the approved manner.

CHARLES WELLS LTD.

The Brewery, Bedford MK40 1QA.
One third of the Wells' tied houses serve 'real ale' — draught IPA and Mild.

YATES AND JACKSON LTD.

8 Brock Street, Lancaster LA1 1UX.
Forty-three tied houses, all within a twenty-five mile radius of Lancaster, serve draught Bitter and Mild from manual or electric bar pumps.

YOUNG AND CO. BREWERY LTD.

The Ram Brewery, Wandsworth, London SW18.

One hundred and forty tied houses, a good many of them in south-west London, and all serving Bitter, Special Bitter, Best Malt Ale and Winter Warmer (occasionally, and only during the winter months). Try Richard I, Royal Hill, London SE10; The Pied Bull, 498 Streatham High Road, London SW16; and one of the newer Young's pubs, The Pig and Whistle, Merton Road, London SW18.

The Home-Brewed Houses

Home-brewed houses are those establishments where the beer is brewed *on the premises* for sale to the public. In the eighteenth century nearly half of all beer produced was brewed in this way. Now there are just six home brewers, but the beer they produce, whether bottled or draught, is the object of lavish praise from those fortunate enough to sample it. We list all six of the home brewers below, together with information on where their beers can be found:

ALL NATIONS INN

Coalport Road, Madeley, Salop. Tel: Telford 585747.
Licensee: Mrs W. H. Lewis.
Brew: Mild Ale.

BLUE ANCHOR INN

Coinage Hall Street, Helston, Cornwall.
Licensee: Mr. Geoffrey Richards.
Brew: Spingo Bitter (in two strengths) and a Winter Brew available at Christmas and Easter.

OLD SWAN BREWERY

Halesowen Road, Netherton, Dudley, West Midlands. Tel: Dudley 53075.
Licensee: Mrs. Pardoe.
Brew: A 'superb bright beer' brewed by Mrs. Pardoe. Also available at The White Swan, Swancote Street, Dudley.

THREE TUNS BREWERY

Bishops Castle, Salop. Tel: 229.
Licensee: John C. E. Roberts.
Brew: A draught Mild and draught XXX.

MINERS ARMS

Priddy, Somerset.

Licensee: Paul Leyton.
Brew: Own Ale (bottled only, but still worth sampling).

TRAQUAIR HOUSE

Inverleithen, Peebles-shire, Scotland.
Licensee: P. Maxwell Stuart.
Brew: A strong Ale. Available from Traquair House. Can also be purchased at Young and Saunders, 5 Queensferry Street, Edinburgh, and in a number of hotels near Edinburgh: Houston House Hotel, Broxburn; Gordon Arms Hotel, Yarrow; Park Hotel, Peebles; Old Mill Inn, Blyth Bridge, Peebles-shire; Howgate Inn, Howgate, nr. Edinburgh; The Old Eagle Inn, Howard Street, Glasgow.

MALT WHISKY

Single malt whisky — not the grain distillation familiar in blended whiskies, nor even the vatted or mixed malts preferred by some — is the grandfather of the whisky clan, the direct descendant of the 'uisge beatha', the water of life, that has probably been distilled in Scotland for more than a thousand years. Nowadays, it is less widely known than other, newer whiskies, consumed by only a very small proportion of whisky drinkers, and certainly much more elusive. And yet it holds a very special place in what anyone might be forgiven for describing as the 'spirit world'.

What is it, then, that makes malt whisky such a distinctive drink? And why should it be singled out for special attention? It is, to begin with, one of the most interesting of the spirits. Its character varies from region to region: Highland malts — those distilled in the area north of an imaginary line stretching from Greenock to Dundee — differ markedly from the Lowland malts produced south of that line; Islay malts, from the island, are considered to be far more 'robust' than Campbeltown malts from the Mull of Kintyre. But these are the elementary distinctions easily discovered and recognised. Of far greater interest to the connoisseur are the subtle differences in character from one distillery to the next within any of the regions. Curiously, each one of the malts has a unique and quite distinctive character, and yet they are all produced in virtually the same way, using the same sort of equipment, the same processes, and the same three ingredients: peat, barley and water.

In the first stages, the barley is screened, soaked in water, or 'steeps', and spread on the malting floor to germinate — a process which takes from eight to twelve days, and is halted at the appropriate moment by drying the green malt over peat fires in a malt kiln. Once dried, the malt is milled to a grist, transferred to a 'mash tun', infused with hot water, converting the by now soluble starch into a sugary liquid known as 'wort'. This, in turn, is drawn off from the 'tun', cooled, and passed to the fermenting vats.

Fermentation takes about 48 hours, after which the 'wash' (a mixture of yeast, crude alcohol, residues and the by-products of fermentation) moves on once more to the first of two pot stills through which it must pass. The 'wash' is heated, or more accurately boiled, over a coal fire or steam-heated coils. The alcohol evaporates off, moving up the neck of the still into the cooling plant, a coiled copper tube known, appropriately, as the 'worm'. Here it recondenses, and the distillates, or low wines as they are called, move on to the spirit still, where the process is repeated for the second and final time. Only about a third of the distillate is passed into the 'spirit receiver', however; the first raw runnings, or foreshots, are returned to the spirit still with the feints, or last runnings, to be mixed with low wines during the next distillation. What the stillman considers to be 'potable spirit', the middle cut, is then stored in oak casks and left to mature.

With only one or two variations (the Springbank distillery, for example, redistills the foreshots and feints in a separate still before returning them to the spirit still to be mixed with low wines), the same procedures are followed in all of the malt distilleries. Stills may vary slightly in size or shape, but most connoisseurs would agree that such differences do not account in full for the marked dissimilarities in flavour. Why is there so much variation?

'Peat reek', the characteristically smoky aroma, is common to all malts: some impart a stronger 'reek' during the drying process than others. The water used during distillation has a great deal to do with the character of the finished product: a source of good, unpolluted soft water is essential to the success of the distilling process, and it is certainly true that distilleries within a mile of each other using water from different burns produce whiskies that are quite different in flavour. The stillman's skill (and the preferences of particular distilleries) in determining the point at which the 'middle cut' should begin and end obviously contributes to the individuality of a particular malt. All of these factors, in combination, obviously play their part in contributing to the unique qualities of the various malts. But the most important factor of all, and the most mysterious, is the presence (and the effect) of certain impurities in the newly distilled spirit. It is unquestionably true that they exist and are far more prevalent in malt whiskies than in the grain whiskies produced in Coffey stills, but no one is quite sure what these impurities are, or what they do. It is possible that they consist of oils from the barley and residues from secondary fermentations which took place after normal fermentation had creased. These 'secondary constituents' react with the air that permeates the oak casks in which the spirit is stored, changing and mellowing the whisky as it matures. And this, in the opinion of a good many whisky enthusiasts, is as much an essential part of the distillation process as any other.

Interestingly, this means that although malt whisky has been produced in the same way for centuries (with a few concessions to the sophistications and conveniences of technology and the Customs and Excise authorities), the malt we drink now has little in common with its historical forebears. For if the rumours are to be believed, malt was originally consumed more or less straight from the barrel, shortly after distillation had been completed. Now, by law, all whiskies – malt or otherwise – must mature for at least three years before they can be sold. In practice very little whisky of any sort is sold before it is five years old. More often than not it finds its way on to the market only after maturing in the cask for eight, ten or twelve years, sometimes longer.

In the case of malt whiskies, however, the market is a confusingly restricted one. Only a certain proportion of the malt produced at any one distillery is actually bottled as a single malt, as much of it (too much, some enthusiasts would say) is used in blending. Very few of the distilleries do their own bottling or distribution; both operations are usually performed by an agent, and it is the latter function, the question of distribution, that most concerns us here. South of the border, in particular, it seems to be erratic. The recent convert, new to the game and anxious to taste as many malts as possible, will find the task of tracking down a particular malt a difficult one. It is probably of little comfort to know that the seasoned enthusiast, preferences firmly established, must confront the same problems. In a way, the hunt is part of the fun: a true connoisseur could never be thrown by such trifles.

If any incentive were needed, whisky *aficionados* are fond of quoting the Scotsman James Hogg, who once claimed that 'if a body could find out the exac' proper proportion and quantity that ought to be drunk and keep to that, I verily trow that he might leeve forever and never die at a', and that doctors and kirkyards would go oot o' fashion'.

SOURCES OF SUPPLY

Information on the various malts is relatively hard to come by. In some cases, the distillers or their agents are perfectly happy to part with the information required, but in other cases it has been almost impossible to persuade the companies concerned to release any details of distribution, in Scotland or the rest of the UK. Where details of stockists have not been included, I would suggest that you write either to the agents or the distillers concerned — they are usually happy to deal with individual queries, as long as they are reasonable requests.

The various malts have been listed alphabetically, although in some cases, more than one malt is bottled or distributed by the company concerned.

ABERLOUR-GLENLIVET
(bottled at nine years old, 70 degrees of proof)

Agents: White Heather Distilleries, 127 Vincent Street, Glasgow C2.
Tel: 041 933 9333.
More than 8,000 of the 13,000 licensed outlets in Scotland are supplied with stocks of Aberlour, on a regular or occasional basis, so it should prove easy to locate north of the border. In England, the situation is less certain. Write to the Scottish agents for further details. It is usually stocked in London by Harrods, Fortnum and Mason, the Soho Wine Market and selected branches of the Wine Market chain.

ARDBEG
(Islay malt)

Distillers: Ardbeg Distillery, 121 St. Vincent Street, Glasgow C2.
Rumour has it that Ardbeg is at its best when around eight years old. That is if you can find it!

AUCHENTOSHAN
(lowland malt, bottled at five years old, 70 degrees of proof)

Agents: Eadie Cairns Ltd., 11 Bothwell Street, Glasgow C2.
Available from the Eadie Cairns off-licence at 91 Hope Street, Glasgow. Write to the agents for details of stockists elsewhere.

AULTMORE
(bottled at 12 years old, 70 degrees of proof)

Agents: John and Robert Harvey, 5 Oswald Street, Glasgow C2.
Tel: 041 332 6022.
Again, probably best to approach the agents direct for information on stockists.

BALBLAIR/MILTONDUFF-GLENLIVET

Agents: Hiram Walker and Sons Ltd., Dunbarton G82 1ND. Tel: 0389 65111.
Balblair only very occasionally bottled as a single malt. Miltonduff-Glenlivet more widely available, bottled at 12 years, 85 degrees of proof.

BALVENIE/GLENFIDDICH

Agents: William Grant and Sons, 208 George Street, Glasgow C2.
Both malts bottled at eight years. Glenfiddich in particular is widely available throughout Scotland and the rest of the UK. In case of difficulty, write to the London agents; William Grant and Sons, 40 Piccadilly, London W1V 9PA (Tel: 01 734 2316).

BLADNOCH

Distillers: Bladnoch Distillery, 5 Claremont Terrace, Glasgow G3 7XR.
A lowland malt from one of the most southerly of Scotland's distilleries. Write to the distillers for further information, should you be unable to obtain it.

BLAIR ATHOL/INCHGOWER/DUFFTOWN GLENLIVET

Agents: Arthur Bell and Sons Ltd., Perth, Scotland. Tel: 0738 2111.
Inchgower (bottled at 12 years, 80 degrees of proof), Blair Athol and Dufftown-Glenlivet (bottled at 8 years, 70 degrees of proof) fairly widely distributed

through larger branches of the Wine Market chain, Peter Dominic, Stowells of Chelsea, Macfisheries (larger supermarkets only, and then not always available). Londoners should be able to find it at larger branches of the London Co-op. supermarkets; The Malt Shop, Scotch House, Knightsbridge; Army and Navy Stores, Victoria, SW1; John Lewis, Oxford Street; Harrods, Knightsbridge; Fortnum and Mason, Piccadilly. In Birmingham, Rackhams usually have small stocks of all three. In Edinburgh, apart from the more familiar specialist outlets, the Woolworths branch in Princes Street has just begun to carry stocks.

BOWMORE/GLEN GARIOCH

Agents: Stanley Morrison (Agencies) Ltd., 5 Royal Crescent, Glasgow G3 7SL. Tel: 041 332 9011.
Both malts available at the following stores throughout the UK: in Anglesey (J. Keegan); Birmingham (Geo. Edwards, branches of Underwoods and Balblake Wines); Bristol (Avery's, Downside Wines, Howells and Morans); Cardiff (Collier and Co.); Cheltenham (L. M. Elston, Galloways); Coventry (Balblake Wines and branches of Moores Wines); Devizes (E. Giddings); Harrogate (E. Standings); Leamington Spa (Thornley Kelsey, Burgis and Colbourne); Leeds (E. Robson); Liverpool (Thos. Baty, J. Sykes, H. King and Co.); London (Bentalls, Block, Grey and Block, Bow Wine Vaults, Bushell Bros., Cameron French, branches of W. H. Cullen, Dolamore, selected branches of Ellis and Co., Fortnum and Mason, Hannells Stores, Harrods, High Brech Vintners, Harvey Bradfield Toyer, Robert Jackson, G. J. Jones, Moore Bros., Selfridges, Sherriffs of London, Ship Wine Company, Soho Wine Market, A. Simon and branches of Winefare); Manchester (Kendal Milne, Willoughby's, Lennon's); Morpeth (W. L. Sanderson); Nottingham (Weavers Wines); Peterborough (E. Crisp); Plymouth (Collier and Co.); Preston (J. Bateson); Rotherham (Fosters of Thryberg); St. Helens (Gallie and Co.); Skegness (Meleyn Moffat); Tavistock (N. Creber); Wakefield (Wakefield Wines); Warrington (G. and J. Greenall); Wolverhampton (Castlecroft Wines).

BRUICHLADDICH/DEANSTON MILL/TULLIBARDINE/TAMNAVULIN-GLENLIVET

Agents: Invergordon Distillers Ltd., 181 West George Street, Glasgow C2. Tel: 041 248 3051.
Bruichladdich can be obtained by mail order from Young and Saunders in Edinburgh. For information on stockists for the remaining three malts, contact the distillers direct.

CARDHU

Agents: John Walker and Sons Ltd., Kilmarnock. Tel: 0563 23401.

In Scotland, Cardhu (bottled at 12 years, 70 degrees of proof) is available from Gordon and Macphail, South Street, Elgin. South of the border, distribution is mainly through the branches of Augustus Barnett. Harrods occasionally have stocks of the malt. Cases can be ordered by the public direct from the English agents: John Walker and Sons, Home Trade Department, St. James's Street, London W1 (Tel: 01 493 8155).

CLYNELISH HIGHLAND MALT

Agents:
Scotland Ainslie and Heilbron (Dist.) Ltd., 5 Oswald Street, Glasgow C1
Tel: 041 221 3254.
England
In England, distribution of Clynelish is handled by the members of the Independent Wine Buyers Consortium, listed below. The nearest agent should be able to supply details of stockists in your area:

J. G. Horton Esq., Wm. Addison (Newport) Ltd., 67 High Street, Newport, Salop (Tel: 095 281 0652)

S. L. C. Medrington Esq., Thomas Baty & Sons Ltd., 37/41 North John Street, Liverpool L2 6SN. (Tel: 051 236 1601)

M. Swatland Esq., Central Wine Buyers (S. Leics.) Ltd., 38 London Road, Oadby, Leics. (Tel: 0533 719121)

J. H. Charlton Esq., Bullingdon House, 2 Butter Market, Thame, Oxon. OX9 3EW (Tel: Thame 2160)

W. M. Stuart Esq., J. & T. Currie, 12 Charles Street, Perth, PH2 8LA (Tel: 0738 24397)

H. P. Dutton Esq., George Dutton & Sons Ltd., Godstall Lane, off St. Werburgh Street, Chester CH1 1LJ (Tel: 0244 21488)

W. J. Hair Esq., Eldridge, Pope & Co. Ltd., Dorchester Brewery, Weymouth Avenue, Dorchester, Dorset DT1 1QT (Tel: Dorchester 4801/4)

D. A. Everton Esq., Evertons of Ombersley Ltd., Worcester Road, Ombersley, nr. Droitwich, Worcestershire WR9 0EW (Tel: 0905 620282)

J. S. Fells Esq., John E. Fells & Sons Ltd., 56/65 Tooley Street, London SE1 2TE (Tel: 01 407 4243)

A. C. George Esq., Goodhews Matthews Ltd., Watermead House, 19-31 Church Street, Epsom, Surrey (Tel: Epsom 26121)

N. H. McNaught Esq., Edwin Giddings, Kennet House, Northgate Street,

Devizes, Wiltshire (Tel: Devizes 3361)

A. Littler Esq., Whitwhams Wines Ltd., Heath Road, Hale, Altrincham, Cheshire (Tel: 061 928 9416)

J. M. Hynard Esq., Hynard Hughes & Co. Ltd., 4 Overton Road, Leicester LE5 0JA (Tel: 0533 769496)

D. Martin Esq., Martin Bros. (Wines & Spirits) Ltd., 292-294 High Street, Cheltenham, Glos. GL50 3HQ

D. T. Platt Esq., Terry Platt (Wines & Spirits) Co., Dysynni House, 14 College Green, Towyn, Gwynedd (Tel: 0654 710389)

D. J. Smith Esq., Seligman & Co. Ltd., 31a Colmore Row, Birmingham B3 2BS (Tel: 021 236 6925)

R. G. Caldicott Esq., Waters of Coventry Ltd., 29 High Street, Coventry, West Midlands (Tel: 0203 26657/8)

J. H. Wells Esq., Charles Wells Ltd., The Brewery, Horne Lane, Bedford MK40 1QA (Tel: 0234 51821)

J. R. Lees-Jones Esq., J. W. Lees & Co. (Brewers) Ltd., Greengate Brewery, Middleton Junction, Manchester M24 2AX (Tel: 061 643 2487)

B. Hildick Esq., Whittalls Wines Ltd., 1-5 Kingsley Street, Walsall, West Midlands WS2 9RB (Tel: 0922 24777/9)

J. D. Rushton Esq., Whitesides of Clitheroe Ltd., Shawbridge Street, Clitheroe, Lancs. BB7 1NA (Tel: Clitheroe 2281)

DALMORE/TOMINTOUL-GLENLIVET/FETTERCAIRN GLENLIVET

Agents: Whyte and Mackay, 50 Wellington Street, Glasgow C2.
Tel: 041 221 4416.
Eight, twelve and twenty year bottlings of all three malts are available in Scotland from selected branches of D. Haddow Ltd. (head office: 164 Killearn Street, Glasgow) or through Gordon and Macphail, South Street, Elgin. In England, all three are distributed by Jarvis Halliday and Co. Ltd. (London office: 62 Pall Mall, London SW1 Tel: 01 930 1778).

GLENDEVERON

Distillers: William Lawson Ltd., 288 Main Street, Coatbridge.
Bottled at five years, 75 degrees of proof. Write to the distillers for further information.

GLENDRONACH

Agents: William Teacher & Sons Ltd., St. Enochs Square, Glasgow.
Bottled at eight years, 80 degrees of proof. Write to the agents for further information on stockists, although it is worth looking for first as there are 'pockets' of distribution scattered round the country.

GLENFARCLAS-GLENLIVET

Distillers: J. and G. Grant, Glenfarclas-Glenlivet Distillery, Badindalloch, Banffshire.
The distillery itself sells eight year bottlings at 80 degrees of proof. Can be found at 15 years and up to 105 degrees. Landmark, of Carrbridge in Inverness-shire sell an eight-year-old, available to mail order customers.

GLEN FLAGLER

Distillers: Inver House Distillers Ltd., 78 St. Vincent Street, Glasgow C2.
Bottled at eight years and five years, 70 degrees of proof. Write to the distillers for further information.

GLENGOYNE

Agents: Lang Bros. Ltd., Dungoyne, Stirlingshire.

GLEN MOHR/OBAN

Distillers: Scottish Malt Distillers, Elgin.
Glen Mohr usually bottled at ten years, 75 degrees of proof and six years, 70 degrees of proof. Write to the distillers for further information on availability.

GLENMORANGIE

Agents: Macdonald and Muir, Queens Dock, Edinburgh EH6 6NN.
Tel: 031 554 5111.
Fairly widely distributed in Scotland, less easily found south of the border. Bottles and half bottles obtainable by mail order from Young and Saunders, Edinburgh.

GLEN SCOTIA

Agents: A. Gillies and Co. Ltd., 4 Newton Place, Glasgow G3 7PE.

GLENTURRET

Agent and distiller: Glenturret Distillery, Crieff, Perthshire. Tel: 0764 2424.

Not very easy to find. Probably a direct approach to the distillery would throw some light on the matter of availability.

HIGHLAND PARK/TANDHU-GLENLIVET

Agents: Hepburn and Ross Ltd., 19-39 Otago Street, Kelvinbridge, Glasgow. Tel: 041 339 7272.
Available from Young and Saunders in Edinburgh, and fairly widely distributed throughout the rest of Scotland. In England, the larger branches of the London Co-op sometimes have both in stock, and it can also be found at Rackhams in Birmingham. Should you experience any difficulty in tracking down a bottle, the agent for England can be reached at 1 Whytingham Road, Thring, Herts. Highland Park (100 degrees proof, 8 years old) can be obtained by mail order from Landmark, Carrbridge, Inverness-shire and from Young and Saunders.

JURA

Agents and distillers: Isle of Jura Distillery, Isle of Jura, Argyll.
Bottled at eight years, 70 degrees of proof, and available occasionally by mail order from Young and Saunders in Edinburgh. For further information on stockists, write to the distillery.

KNOCKANDO

Agents: Justerini and Brooks, 39 George Street, Edinburgh. Tel: 031 226 4202.
Available direct from Justerini and Brooks at the above address. They can also supply further information on outlets in Scotland. In England, the whisky can be bought from their branch at 61 St. James' Street, London SW1, who can also advise on availability outside London. Distribution is fairly widespread, but tends to be a little erratic.

LAGAVULIN

Agents: White Horse Distillers Ltd., Barron Street, Glasgow G4 9XF.
An Islay malt, available by mail order and to personal shoppers at Landmark, Carrbridge, Inverness-shire, at twelve years old, 75 degrees of proof.

LAPHROAIG/TORMORE

Distillers: Long John Distillers Ltd., 55 Blythswood Street, Glasgow G2.
Ten-year-old Laphroaig, an Islay malt, is available from Young and Saunders, who can fill orders for mail order customers. In London it can occasionally be found at Fortnums and Harrods.

LINKWOOD

Agents: John McEwan and Co. Ltd., Leith

LONGMORN GLENLIVET/GLEN GRANT/GLENLIVET

Agents:
Scotland Glenlivet Distillers Ltd., 45 Frederick Street, Edinburgh.
Tel: 031 226 6581.
England Matthew Clark and Sons Ltd., 183 Central Street, London EC1.
Tel: 01 253 7646.
In Scotland, all three malts are obtainable from Chivas Bros., 387 Union Street, Aberdeen; Eadie Cairns, 91 Hope Street, Glasgow; Charles Muirhead, 63 George Street, Edinburgh EH2; Gordon and MacPhail, South Street, Elgin. In England, Rackhams in Birmingham and Chiesmans in Canterbury (and other branches) have stocks of Glenlivet and ten-year-old Glen Grant. Fortnum and Mason, Piccadilly have Glenlivet and stocks of a five-year-old Glen Grant. Harrods and Selfridges (Knightsbridge and Oxford Street respectively) both have stocks of five-year-old Glen Grant. The latter can also be obtained by mail order from Young and Saunders in Edinburgh and Landmark in Carrbridge.

MORTLACH GLENLIVET

Distillers: Mortlach Distillery, Dufftown, Banffshire.
Bottles of 70 degrees of proof, twelve-year-old Mortlach can be supplied by mail order from Landmark in Carrbridge.

ORD

Agents: Peter Dawson Ltd., 75 Hope Street, Glasgow C2. Tel: 041 221 7111.
In England Ord is distributed through Tollemache and Cobbolt, the East Anglian brewery (head office: Cliff Brewery, Ipswich, Tel: 0473 56751) and is available at the following branches of Barwells: 94 Rushmere Road, Ipswich; 16 Charing Cross, Norwich; 48-50 Bridge Street, Lodden, Norfolk; 28 Carlton Road, Lowestoft, Suffolk; 148 Kings Street, Great Yarmouth, Norfolk; 15 Eastgate Street, Bury St. Edmunds, Suffolk; 41 Head Street, Colchester, Essex; 2 London Road, Clacton, Essex; 21 High Street, Brightlington, Essex; The Cross Inn, Woodbridge, Suffolk; 25 Ranelagh Road, Felixstowe; 145 Connaught Avenue, Frinton-on-Sea, Essex; 68 Trumpington Street, Cambridge; 3 Reddenham Road, Harlesden, Norfolk; 157 Queens Road, Buckhurst Hill, Essex; 40 Market Place, North Walsham, Norfolk; 8 Dixons Fold, Old Catton, Norwich; and 13 Queen Street, Haverhill, Suffolk. All of the above branches should either carry stocks or be able to order supplies at fairly short notice.

ROSEBANK

Agents: Distillers Agency Ltd., 63 Pall Mall, London SW1. Tel: 01 930 6556. In London, only available with any regularity from the Ship Wine Co., 46 Beak Street, W1 (Tel: 01 437 1345) and the Soho Wine Market, 3 Greek Street, London W1 (Tel: 01 437 9311).

SPRINGBANK

Distillers: J. and A. Mitchell, Springbank Distillery, Campbeltown, Argyllshire. Distillery-bottled at twelve years, 80 degrees of proof. The malt, a Campbeltown one, can also be obtained at eight years, 80 degrees of proof by mail order from Young and Saunders in Edinburgh.

STRATISTHLA-GLENLIVET

Agents: Chivas Bros., 11 Renfrew Road, Paisley.
Write direct to the agents for further details of stockists.

TALISKER

Distillers: Dailmain-Talisker Distilleries Co., 1 Trinity Road, Elgin, Morayshire. Bottled at 70, 80 and occasionally 100 degrees of proof. Bottles of 80 degrees of proof are available to mail order customers from Young and Saunders in Edinburgh. Write to the distillery for further details of distribution.

TOMATIN

Agents: Tomatin Distillers Co. Ltd., 34 Dover Street, London W1.
Tel: 01 629 9592.
Bottled at five and ten years old, and only very limited quantities available on the home market. Obtainable through the agents at the address given. In Scotland, contact H. D. Wines (Inverness) Ltd., Longman Road, Inverness, for further information on stockists north of the border.

In general the following suppliers can normally supply most of the malts described. Sadly, they are few and far between, but are well worth a visit:

W. Milroy, 46 Beak Street, London W1.

Fortnum and Mason, Piccadilly, London W1.

Gordon and Macphail, 58-60 South Street, Elgin IV30 1JY, Scotland.

Strachan of Royal Deeside, Station Square, Aboyne, Scotland.

C. Muirhead and Son, 63 George Street, Edinburgh EH2.

ENGLISH WINES: WINE-GROWING IN ENGLAND

Major-General Sir Guy Salisbury-Jones, GCVO, CMG, CBE, MC

History

Wine-growing in Great Britain is not a new venture. In AD 280 the Emperor Probus authorised Britain to cultivate the vine and to make wine. After that date viticulture in Britain continued with various degrees of intensity until the end of the eighteenth century. The greatest setback occurred when Henry VIII dissolved the Monasteries; ever since that time, there has been a prejudice against home-grown wine. In 1789, for example, The Hon. Charles Hamilton, who owned a vineyard in Surrey, wrote thus: 'Many good judges of wine were deceived by my wine, and thought it superior to any Champagne they ever drank; but such is the prejudice of most people against anything of English growth, I generally found it most prudent not to declare where it grew till after they had passed their verdict upon it.' Successive generations of British wine-growers have had to contend with that same prejudice.

Hambledon Vineyard

I think that the idea of planting a vineyard was born on a Flanders battlefield in 1917. On a cold wet day in that year we attacked alongside the French. On reaching our objective, we found ourselves wallowing in mud alongside some French soldiers. Taking pity on us, they shared with us their wine ration, and on that day was born my love not only for France, but for her wine. Love of wine blossomed into an interest in wine-growing and more than thirty years later, in 1952, inspired by the writings of Edward Hyams and Barrington Brock, I decided to make the experiment of planting a vineyard at Hambledon. I therefore set forth with our gardener, Mr. Blackman, for the vineyards of Burgundy to have a look round. With us we took a sack of our chalky Hampshire soil with a view to its analysis and the choice of the most suitable vines. It so happened that our visit coincided with a banquet given by the Confrerie des Chevaliers du Tastevin at the former Cistercian Monastery of Clos-Vougeot. To this banquet we were both bidden, and I have often thought since that it was under the influence of Burgundian hospitality that I ordered 4,000 vines. The vine recommended was the Seyve-Villard 5.276 (now called Seyval). All these were grafted on American rootstock in order to enable them to resist phylloxera. The rootstock recommended as being the most suitable for our soil was 161.49. We were now committed.

Until the vines had been planted, I had given little serious consideration to the problems involved, but I soon came to respect that French writer who once described the vine as the most exacting mistress in the world. Indeed, she demands much money to be established and much money and labour to maintain.

Equipment Required

Apart from the initial cost of the vines, much equipment will be required for their cultivation. This includes posts and wire to support them, a tractor with attachments for hoeing and spraying, rabbit wire to surround the vineyard and harvesting equipment such as secateurs, trugs and containers. Moreover, since no effective birdscarer has yet been devised, only the use of netting can give real peace of mind. In considering the cost of this equipment, it should be borne in mind that it is not until the third year after planting that one ounce of juice, or 'must' as it is called, will be available for wine-making; in the meantime, annual expenditure will already be required in respect of wages, fertilisers, and other items.

If it is decided to press the grapes and to make, bottle and store the wine on the estate, additional capital expenditure will be required for the purchase of such items as a grape-mill, a press, fermentation and maturing vats, filtering and bottling equipment, and a labelling machine. Moreover, unless suitable buildings already exist for the purpose, a winery and cellar will have to be built. In so far as annual expenditure is concerned the main items to be considered are sugar, fining material, bottles, corks and labels and, last but not least, excise duties.

Labour

Labour in the vineyard is almost continuous throughout the year. Immediately after the harvest, at the end of October or beginning of November, there takes place what the French call the 'Butage'. This entails ploughing a furrow between each row of vines, thus throwing up the earth to cover the graft on each vine. Special attachments to the tractor are required for this purpose. Fortunately, in November and December, when there is much work to be done in the winery, work in the vineyard is mainly limited to manuring. However, from January until the harvest the vines need constant attention. In January it is advisable to start pruning, and this operation may well continue until the beginning of April. The vines then have to be tied to the wires and this operation may continue into May. Throughout the summer there is rarely a dull moment: hoeing, disbudding, spraying against insect and fungus diseases, and summer pruning are just a few of the operations involved. As a result of experiments now being conducted on the Continent with various weed-killing products, a measure of the labour now required in the vineyard may be reduced. At the end of September the nets are put over the vines and the resultant lull affords a little time to enable preparations to be made for the harvest.

Even in a bad year when the crop is poor, we generally succeed in making the harvest an appropriately joyful occasion. Indeed, long before it becomes wine, the grape tends to radiate gaiety. We fill the house with young people and friends from the village.

Wine-Making

Once the grapes have been gathered, attention can be switched from viticulture to wine-making or vinification, as it is called. On the advice of our French friends we only make a white wine. Normally, a good red wine can only be made in a more southern climate. The equipment required for wine-making has been referred to above. The actual process of wine-making can only be touched upon briefly, for its production requires a combination of art and skill and much experience. After the grapes have been pressed, the must is allowed to rest for about twelve hours in order to allow the heaviest of the unwanted ingredients to settle at the bottom. This in fact is the first stage of fining. On the following day the must is pumped into fermentation vats, and at this stage, in most years, sugar must be added in order to ensure that the wine will have an alcoholic strength of about 11½ per cent; a suitable wine yeast is also added. Fermentation then continues until just before Christmas, when the must will have become wine. It is then racked off into maturing vats where it will remain until the following spring when it is bottled. Before bottling, however, the wine is fined by the use of a product known as Bentonite. After three months in bottle the wine is drinkable, but it should be at its best after three years, after which it is unlikely to improve.

I am often asked what our wine is like. I have already said that we only make a white wine. I once asked one of my Burgundian friends, very distinguished in the wine world, whether he thought we should ever be able to produce an acceptable wine. Witty and cautious was his reply — 'Men' he said, 'are as fickle with wine as they are with women. Sometimes they love "une grande dame", but from time to time they prefer "une petite femme frivole".' At the outset our wine may have been a little frivolous, but since then it has acquired more noble qualities. Indeed, only a few weeks ago, as the result of a sample bottle we had sent to Germany, we received an order to export 100 cases to that country. If further evidence be needed that prejudice against English wine is declining, I might mention that a few months ago I received a letter from a world famous wine-grower in Bordeaux, which started thus: 'Mon cher Général et cher Collègue'.

This letter gave me exceptional pleasure. Even our French friends were beginning to take us seriously!

Viability

Our experience over more than twenty years has convinced me that the minimum area that is viable is five acres. Anything less would hardly justify the expensive tractor and other equipment which I have mentioned above. As the following figures will show, the rough cost of establishing such a vineyard would be about £18,000:

15,000 vines (grafted)	£ 6,000
Viticultural equipment	£ 2,500
Wine-making equipment	£ 6,000
3 years wage bill	£ 3,600
Total:	£18,100

Although cheaper equipment could be obtained, I think it advisable to make a high estimate, on the assumption that in the long run the most up-to-date equipment will prove the most economical.

The annual cost of running such a vineyard, which will include such items as fertilisers, wages, fixed farm costs, cultivation and harvest equipment, and administrative expenses, including excise duties and depreciation, will amount to about £9,000. Since the annual average production will probably not exceed 12,000 bottles, it will be seen that the minimum retail price per bottle must be over £1 in order to produce a profit.

Since much of the expenditure and labour involved is attributable to the equipment and labour required for wine-making, a co-operative scheme is now being developed by Mr. Jack Ward of the Merrydown Wine Company, whereby the viticulturalist can concentrate on the vineyard only and sell his grapes to the central co-operative for pressing and processing. This solution, which is common in many parts of France, is proving very attractive to some English wine-growers and is a less formidable project than to combine both the growing of grapes and the making of wine.

Before leaving the all-important question of viability, I would like to consider in passing the two outstanding factors which militate against it – firstly, the weather, and secondly, the excessive excise duties. While the one is unpredictable, the other can be remedied by a sympathetic Chancellor. On the very day these lines are being written these duties have just been greatly raised. We are therefore placed in the ludicrous position of having to seek export outlets. With regard to the weather, it so happens that in the last three years, two harvests have been adversely affected as the result of rain during the critical period of flowering at the beginning of July. Two bad years out of three are obviously unacceptable, but it seems most unlikely that over a long period such a dismal average would persist.

Conclusion

In spite of persistent prejudice, we have now gained sufficient experience to affirm not only that viticulture in Britain is practicable, but that the wine can be of high quality. We are now concentrating on quality, and with that object in view, although the Seyval has produced good wine, we are gradually increasing the percentage of more noble vines, such as the Pinot Noir, the Chardonnay, and the Pinot Meunier; all these vines are used in the production of Champagne, where the chalky soil is similar to our own. The membership of the English Vineyards Association is rapidly increasing and there are now nearly 400 acres of vines in Great Britain.

I cannot emphasise too strongly that the cultivation of the vine is a serious business. Voltaire said that he 'knew of nothing really serious here below except the cultivation of the vine'. If, therefore, it is decided to espouse the vine, it should not be taken in hand, 'unadvisedly, lightly or wantonly'. For example, it would be inadvisable to plant a vineyard in the absence of a suitable site and soil. Of the two, the site is the more important, for up to a point, the soil can be adjusted. Speaking generally, the most suitable site is a southern or south-easterly slope, clear of frost pockets. I would also emphasise that in view of the highly specialised nature both of viticulture and of vinification it would be inadvisable not to seek expert advice in both fields, preferably from the Continent. For example, we are in constant communication with a highly qualified wine-grower in Champagne who comes over to help us; and in the field of vinification we have the advice of a German wine chemist who is now established in this country.

If I have highlighted the difficulties of wine-growing in this country, it is because I have been reluctant to lead people astray through over-enthusiasm. But I must conclude on a more cheerful note, for apart from financial considerations the rewards are many. Life is surely incomplete without some link with the soil, and what better link than that 'Prince of Plants', the vine?

But not only is the vine a link with the soil; it provides also a link with that indescribable world of wine. In the words of Georges Duhamel of the French Academy, 'Wine, even before it is drunk, is the true and respectable symbol of Communion between highly civilised people'. Moreover, in most wine-growing countries of the world we now have a footing, and the pleasure of visiting France has been doubled by the contacts we have established in her wine-growing regions. At banquets in Burgundy I have listened enthralled as wine after wine has been praised with superlative eloquence and wit. In the Bordelais, as a Compagnon du Bon Temps Medoc, on entering any cellar, I am in theory entitled to a salute of twelve bangs of a mallet on a wine cask. I have already referred to the advice we receive from Champagne, and we have a very friendly relationship also with the Champagne House of Pol Roger. Such have been but a few of the rewarding compensations for our efforts.

THE VINEYARDS

PILTON MANOR VINEYARD

The Manor House, Pilton, Shepton Mallet, Somerset BA4 4BE.
Tel: Pilton 325.
The vineyard is currently producing two dry white wines: Somerset Riesling Sylvaner and Somerset Seyve Villard. Both are available direct from the vineyard (which is open from Monday to Friday throughout the year) and from the following outlets: Averys of Bristol, 7 Park Street Viaduct, Bristol BS1 5NG; Morans of Bristol, 42 Welsh Back, Bristol 1; Army and Navy Stores, Victoria Street, London SW1; The Ebury Wine Co., 139 Ebury Street, London SW1; Johnson-Peonsgen and Co., 22 Buckingham Gate, London SW1E 6LB; Ellis Son and Vidler, 4 Old Park Lane, London W1; Merrydown Wine Co., Horam Manor, Horam, nr. Heathfield, Sussex.

KENTISH VINEYARDS

Cherry Hill, Nettlestead Green, Wateringbury, Kent. Tel: Maidstone 812655. Kentish Sovereign, White and Rose, currently in production. Can be ordered by the case direct from the vineyard, or through the Agents: Saccone and Speed (head office: 32 Sackville Street, London W1, Tel: 01 734 2061).

HAMBLEDON VINEYARDS LTD.

Mill Down, Hambledon, Portsmouth, Hampshire PO7 6RY. Tel: Hambledon 475. A dry white wine. Available from selected branches of Peter Dominic: 2 Orange Street, London WC2; 127 High Street, Winchester, Hants.; 49 Above Bar, Southampton, Hants.; and 27 East Street, Chichester, Sussex. Also available from Ellis Son and Vidler, 29 White Rock, Hastings, Sussex.

FELSTAR

The Vineyards, Cricks Green, Felsted, Essex. Tel: Great Leighs 504.
The vineyard produces a range of wines, not all of them widely available: Madeleine Sylvaner, Madeleine Angevine, Seyval Blanc, Pinto Selection, Rose, Muller Thurgau, Muscat Selection, Muller Thurgau & Sieger and Reichensteiner formed the 1973 vintage, although there will be variations on this in

subsequent vintages. All are obtainable by the case direct from the vineyard, or from Ingletons Wines Ltd., in Malden, Essex. Harrods also have some of the Felstar wines in stock, and they are occasionally available through selected branches of the Peter Dominic chain, and through Saccone and Speed (see Pilton Manor Vineyard for the address of their head office).

ROCK LODGE VINEYARD

Rock Lodge, Scaynes Hill, nr. Haywards Heath, Sussex. Tel: 044 486 224.
The vineyard, which is now in its fifth year of production on a commercial scale, produces a dry white wine, Rock Lodge Riesling Sylvaner. It can be ordered by the case direct from the vineyard, and is stocked at the Merrydown Wine Shop, at Horam Manor.

GAMLINGAY VINEYARD

Gamlingay, nr. Sandy, Beds. Tel: 50795.
A young vineyard just beginning to produce on a commercial scale. The wine, a dry white Riesling, can be purchased direct from the vineyard by the case, and can be sampled at the University Arms Hotel and the Arts Theatre Restaurant in Cambridge, and the Duncombe Arms Inn, Waresley, Beds.

CAVENDISH MANOR WINE

Nether Hall, Cavendish, Suffolk CO10 8BX. Tel: Glemsford 280221.
The vineyard produces a medium dry Riesling Sylvaner type wine, which can be bought from W. J. Cutting Ltd., High Street, Cavendish, Sudbury, Suffolk, or by appointment from the vineyard itself (by the case).

BIDDENDEN VINEYARDS

Little Whatmans, Biddenden, Ashford, Kent TN27 8DH. Tel: 0580 291237.
The wine, a dry white moselle-type wine, is available from the vineyard itself and from the village shop in Biddenden and the local restaurant, marketed under the label of Biddenden Vineyards Ltd.

ADGESTONE VINEYARD

Sandown, Isle of Wight PO36 0HN. Tel: 098 372 207.
The 1973 Vintage, now available, is fairly widely distributed throughout the south-east under the Adgestone label. Harrods, in London, Oddbins (head office: St. Johns Wharves, 73 Wapping High Street, E1, Tel: 01 481 2944), Berry Bros. and Rudd Ltd. (head office: St. James's Street, London SW1, Tel: 01 930 1888). and Bow Wine Vaults, 10 Bow Chyd, London EC4 (Tel: 01 248 1121) all stock

the wine. In Birmingham, it is available from R. E. Talbois, 171 Broad Street, Edgbaston and in Manchester from Adomvire Wines, c/o Wine Trend, 117 Burton Road, Woodington. For details of retail outlets in other parts of the country, contact the shippers: Deinhard and Co. Ltd., 29 Addington Street, London SE1 7XT (Tel: 01 261 1111), who should be able to supply the relevant details. The wine is not available direct from the vineyard at present.

WOOTTON VINEYARDS

North Town House, North Wootton, Shepton Mallet, Somerset BA4 4AG.
Tel: Pilton 359.
Three wines are produced at the vineyard, all of the dry white Hock type: Seyval, Muller Thurgau and Schonburger, all 1974 vintage. The wines can be bought direct from the vineyard, in single bottles or by the case. The latter can also be sent to private buyers unable to reach the vineyard itself, although it is well worth making the trip as visitors are welcome, and wine tastings can be arranged by appointment – a number of wines from other British vineyards are stocked in the cellar.

THE VINEYARD

Stragglethorpe Hall, Lincoln, Tel: Loveden 72308.
The wine, a dry white wine sold under the Lincoln Imperial label, is fairly widely distributed throughout the East Midlands, particularly in Lincolnshire and Nottinghamshire. Information on the nearest retail stockist can be obtained from the agents, Skinner Rook and Chambers Ltd., 132 Church Street, Eastwood, Nottinghamshire.

NEW HALL VINEYARDS

New Hall, Purleigh, Chelmsford, Essex. Tel: 062 185 343.
One of the largest of the commercial vineyards, established in 1970 and expecting to produce nearly 25,000 bottles of wine in 1975. The three types of wine currently available (all 1974 vintage) are described as 'English white table wines': Muller Thurgau/Reichensteiner, Huxelrebe and Perle. All available in single bottles or by the case direct from the vineyard, or from Lay and Wheeler, Culver Street, Colchester (Tel: Colchester 79551).

THE ISLE OF ELY VINEYARD

Wilburton, Cambridgeshire.
The wine, only in its second year of commercial production, is a dry, white moselle-type wine marketed under the label St. Etheldreda. It is available the Merrydown Wine Shop, at Horam Manor in Sussex, and can also be bought

in single bottles or by the case direct from the vineyard (all enquiries should be directed to N. J. Sneesby, 17 Luard Road, Cambridge CB2 2PJ).

BREDE VINEYARD

Reyson Oasts, Broad Oak, Rye, Sussex.
Two wines — Brede Riesling Sylvaner and Brede Seyve Villard — available from the Post Office Stores, Broad Oak, Rye and the Merrydown Wine Shop, Heathfield, Horam in Sussex. Also available by the case direct from the vineyard.

SOURCES OF SUPPLY

Rather than try to list the ever-growing number of wine shippers and buyers, I thought it more useful simply to mention the grandfather of them all — The Wine Society. Founded just over a hundred years ago as a registered Co-operative Society, it is owned and controlled by its members. Membership is by election, and it is necessary to be proposed for membership by an existing member. Once elected a member receives regular wine lists detailing the various wines and spirits available. In 1975 over 100 different Clarets were offered to members, and a correspondingly wide choice of red and white Burgundies and German wines. Choice within each of the various categories — Port, Sherry, Claret, Burgundy, Champagne, Gin, Whisky, Liqueurs and Vermouth — is enormous, and is generally considered by non-members and members alike to represent extremely good value. Further details of membership can be obtained from the company's London office: 52 Bolsover Street, London W1P 7HL. The company's headquarters are at Gunnels Wood Road, Stevenage, Herts. SG1 2BG.

Coffee, Tea and Tisanes

COFFEE

R. Whittard

'Coffee should be black as the devil, hot as hell, pure as an angel and sweet as love.'
Talleyrand.

To obtain the cup of perfect coffee, many factors have to be considered. Freshness of grind and roast are the first essentials. Most coffee drinkers now possess their own coffee grinders, and they know that no more should be ground than is necessary for immediate use. If no grinder is available, ground coffee should be bought in the smallest quantities possible from a good grocer who roasts his own coffees, or from your nearest coffee specialist, where coffee roasting is a constant daily feature. The roasted coffee beans must be ground to suit the requirements of the method used to make the coffee, and where machines such as Espresso, Cona, Filters, Percolators, etc., are used, the manufacturer's instructions must be closely followed. All coffee-making methods have their advantages and disadvantages, but most experts in the coffee trade will always agree that the jug method is the simplest, and that it gives excellent results when a little care is taken. Using the jug method, the grind can be varied according to the maker's choice: coarsely ground good coffee will give a light flavourful cup with a pronounced aroma, while a finer grind will be less aromatic and stronger, and the finest ground, or pulverised, will be thick, even 'muddy' in the cup, a condition preferred by some. It is important that, whatever method is used, scrupulous cleanliness be observed, particularly with machines where coffee comes into contact with metal. Coffee leaves a small deposit, which after a while will affect subsequent brews of coffee and will sour them; this deposit can be removed by a weak acid solution of a few drops of vinegar in warm water. It is also important, after the coffee has been made, that it be not kept at too high a temperature; it will slowly evaporate and the liquor remaining becomes stronger and more bitter.

The second great essential for coffee perfection is freshness of roast. Coffee in its green, raw state changes slightly and slowly as it ages, but, once roasted, the natural moisture has been expelled and the roasted bean, being porous, is susceptible to atmospheric moisture, with fatal results to its subsequent flavour in the cup. In addition, the aromatic properties of coffee, once developed by roasting, are volatile and rapidly lost when the roasted beans are exposed to air. Therefore, immediate airtight protection is of the greatest importance.

Deterioration of ground coffee is, of course, still more rapid, the many small particles of a coffee bean permitting the loss of aroma and the absorption of moisture to a much greater degree. Therefore, coffee, in bean form or ground, must always be kept as airtight as possible.

The degree to which coffee is roasted is also of importance to the coffee connoisseur. For instance, in hard water areas a full to high Continental roast will give best results, but in softer water districts, lighter and medium roasts will bring out more flavour. Different coffee growths will, of course, vary, but generally speaking lighter to medium roasts will give good aroma and flavour in the cup, the medium to full roasts more strength and thickness in the cup; while the full to high Continental roasts will have lost the typical aroma and bouquet so liked in Britain, but will have gained great strength and blackness, and a pleasantly different, slightly charred flavour, which is much in favour in France. Basically, more coffee is required for the lighter roasts and less for the darker, blacker ones.

Having chosen his method of making coffee, the grind required, and the degree of roast he prefers, the connoisseur now has a variety of growths from which to select. Not all are available all of the time, but most should be found at the good grocer or one of the specialist coffee shops, or one of the mail order coffee specialists. There are two main groups of coffee, the Arabicas and the Robustas. The Arabicas are the coffees of the plantations, mostly of good quality with mild, aroma-full character; the Robustas are the strong, coarse, native-produced and wild coffees mostly from the African forests, and are the lowest priced of all.

Dealing with Arabicas first:

JAMAICA Blue Mountain is usually considered the best for choice aroma, flavour and quality, but, alas, very expensive, in very short supply, and virtually not imported direct into Britain in the last few years. Lower grown Jamaicas do not compare in quality, being at best a neutral coffee with no outstanding feature.

COSTA RICA is a fragrant coffee, the best from Central America, rich in flavour, with some acidity. Those from the Pacific side are of better quality than those from the Atlantic side, but most Costa Ricas can be recommended for a choice, pleasant cup. A favourite breakfast blend might be two parts Costa Rica with one part Kenya.

GUATEMALA, MEXICO, SALVADOR, NICARAGUA, PANAMA, HONDURAS, all produce coffees similar in quality to the Costa Ricas, with choice aroma and richness in the cup, but on the whole not so good and therefore less expensive.

COLOMBIA produces a full bodied coffee, suave and creamy, with less acidity than the Central Americas. It has become popular in Britain over the past few years, and takes a full roast very well.

BRAZIL is the greatest coffee-producing country of all, accounting for probably one-third of world production, and as a consequence the great factor regulating the world price of coffee. The liquor is thick, strong, almost coarse flavoured, not very aromatic, and the least acid of all coffees; it is ideal for full and high Continental roasts. Brazils will sometimes be found in shops as Santos, one of the ports from which the coffee is shipped.

MOCHA coffee is named from the silted-up port on the Red Sea from which both the South Arabian 'Shortberry' and the Ethiopian 'Longberry' coffees were formerly shipped. The Yemeni Shortberry is now virtually unknown in Britain, but there is plenty of the heavier, less delicate Ethiopian Longberry. The liquor has a unique, pronounced flavour, described as 'gamey' or 'cheesey', which is too pungent and too distinctive for many. But carefully controlled, it adds richness to a blend. It is also ideal for making the pulverised Turkish coffee.

MYSORE, and the other coffees from India, Coorg, Naidoobatum, Shevaroys, Nilghiri, etc., are all fairly similar in quality. The Mysores are rich, smooth and creamy with some acidity and good aroma. Coorgs tend to be coarse in the cup, the Naidoobatums above Coorgs in quality. These Indians will take a full roast very well, and when blended with Mocha will make a very pleasant after-dinner coffee, particularly for those who do not like the full, black, Continental roasts.

JAVA AND INDONESIA. The famous 'Old Brown' Java coffee, guaranteed ten years old by the former Dutch Government, frequently wormholed (which enhanced its value), is regretfully a thing of the past. It was noted for its great richness, with an absence of all bitterness and acidity. The present regime is sending over a quite mellow plantation coffee, not up to the standard and quality of the 'Old Brown', but giving a liquor with mild acidity and little or no bitterness.

KENYA produces high-grade, good quality coffees which are excellent for aroma and flavour, with a pleasant acidity and sharpness. They are good on their own and very useful for imparting more flavour and 'bite' to other coffees. They do tend to be light in the cup, however, and this cannot be offset with roasting to a higher degree, because they then become unpleasantly pungent and almost sour. Recommended, therefore, as a light to medium roast coffee, made extravagantly with plenty of coffee, and served with cream, when the true coffee bouquet will be obtained.

TANZANIA coffee is similar to the Kenyas, with equally good quality, but usually lighter in the cup, with fine aroma and good flavour.

NEW GUINEA coffees have improved over the past few years and are being imported in increasing quantities into Britain. They are not unlike the East African coffees in character with less acidity than the Kenyas, and, except for the best, with less flavour.

The above coffees are all 'Arabicas' or mild-flavoured. There are other Arabicas, such as Santo Domingo, Haiti, Venezuela, Bugishu (Uganda), Kivu, Ruanda, etc., but those coffees only come to Britain infrequently and are therefore not likely to be available except occasionally from a coffee specialist.

The other large group of coffees is the Robusta. The coffee tree is indigenous to Africa, growing wild in its tropical forests. The product is quite different from the cultivated coffees of the plantations, which have been improved upon and transplanted around the world from their ultimate origin in Southern Arabia or in Ethiopia. Robusta coffees are imported into Britain from Uganda, Nigeria, Ghana, Sierra Leone, Togo, and Angola in Africa, and from Indonesia. It comes both as washed and unwashed coffee, and being the least expensive of all, is in demand as a price reducer. All have a strong, coarse flavoured liquor; there is little aroma, and none of the real coffee bouquet. Some are better than others with less of the coarse flavour, such as the Indonesians and the Angolans. All should be very fully to highly roasted. But on the whole the Robustas are not to be recommended to would-be connoisseurs.

One particular grade of coffee should be mentioned — the Peaberry. It is produced in every growth of coffee and is the failure of one member of the twin-embryo of the normal double berry pod. There is said to be a gain in nutrients to the remaining member, with consequent increase in the final quality. Peaberry is not so easy to obtain in Britain now, but occasionally the connoisseur will find good ones from Kenya, perhaps from Costa Rica. The coffee is highly desirable, with full flavoured liquor and fine aroma.

Now, knowing a little about the various coffees, the connoisseur must endeavour to perfect his coffee, to find the quality and flavour most suitable for his own palate and taste. He must experiment with mixtures and blends; he will find that ¼ part Kenya added to ¾ parts Brazil will give more briskness than the Brazil on its own, that a blend ½ part high roast and ½ part medium roast (known to some as 'Light and Dark'), will have both strength and flavour, and so on. He will try adding a little fig in the Viennese manner, thereby enriching the liquor and removing some bitterness. He will add chicory to impart more strength and piquancy. He will add cream, or he will drink it black. He will find that a palate can become tired of the same always, and that it pays to have variations every so often.

SOURCES OF SUPPLY

ALGERIAN COFFEE STORES LTD.

52 Old Compton Street, London W1V 6PB. Tel: 01 437 2480.
Eleven different blends of coffee available by mail order or to personal customers: four medium roasts (Java, Boston, Connoisseur and Gourmet Mulatto); full roast

(Mocha Parfait); high roasts (Esotico, Velluto Nero, Algerian Special, Gourmet Noir, Brunette and Sans Pareil). Minimum mail order quantities: 1 lb. Can be sold as ground, but the store prefers to sell beans, as they believe that only freshly ground coffee produces the best results.

H. R. HIGGINS (COFFEE MAN) LTD.

42 South Molton Street, London W1Y 2BD. Tel: 01 629 3913/499 5912.
Higgins usually have in stock thirty different varieties of coffee, of varying roasts and blends, with fifteen 'original' or unblended coffees. Both the blended coffees (Kenyarobi, Brazilia, Grosvenor, Regal, Standard Chagga, Colombian, Breakfast, After-Dinner, Mocha and Mysore, Vienna, Hanover, Santiago, Creole, Sultan and Continental) and the 'original' coffees (Kibo Chagga, Double A Chagga, Standard Costa Rica, Mark H. T. Costa Rica, Mysore, Colombian Medellin, Colombian Libano, Mocha, Bourbon Santos, Santos, Standard Kenya, Kenya Peaberry, Santo Domingo, Java and El Salvador) are available, freshly ground, to mail order customers. Minimum order: ½ lb.

WHITTARD AND CO. LTD.

111 Fulham Road, London SW3 6RP. Tel: 01 589 4261.
Whittards will post (and obviously sell to personal shoppers), the following coffees, which they rank in descending order of strength: After Dinner Pure, Santos and Java (both high roast Continental); Columbia, Half and Half blend, Mocha and Mysore, Pure Coffee with Mocha Mysore, Pure Mocha and Pure African (all strong, medium roast coffees); 'Good Pure Coffee', Choice Pure Coffee, Central American, Costa Rica, Kenya Blend, Kenya, Carribbean Mountain Blend, Brazilian, and Coffee and Chicory Mixture (medium strength and roast). All can be ordered either ground or as beans. The shop also stock pure ground roasted chicory, and pure ground roasted figs, for those customers who want to blend their own flavourings with their coffee.

YOUNG AND SAUNDERS LTD.

5 Queensferry Street, Edinburgh EH2 4PD. Tel: 031 225 6075.
Roast their own coffees daily, and grind as required the following varieties: Breakfast Blend, Shandwick, Yosan No. 1, Yosan No. 2, Continental, Ferry Blend, Mocha, Kenya, Pacific Costa Rica, Mysore and Mountain Blend. All available, ground only, to personal shoppers and by mail order.

BUYBULK LTD.

Tunnel Road, Bourne, Lincs. Tel: Bourne 3291.
Sell to mail order customers (or for collection from their warehouse) their own

branded coffee beans (Continental, East African, Brazilian and Four Nations), a Viennese Blend and a Coffee and Chicory mixture, in larger quantities from 2 lb. upwards.

MARKOS COFFEE CO.

13 Connaught Street, London W2. Tel: 01 723 4020.
Blended coffees, listed in ascending order of strength, and unblended coffees available freshly roasted to personal shoppers and mail order customers: Breakfast, Vienna, Household and Three Star (pale roast); After Dinner, Gourmet, Luxor and Regent (medium roast); Continental Stambul, Negresco (high roast). Unblended coffees available: Santos, Mocha, Mysore, Mocha and Mysore, Kenyan, Tanzanian, Mexican, Jamaican, Colombian, Costa Rican, Old Java, Guatemalan and Brazil de Luxe.

L. FERN AND CO. LTD.

27 Rathbone Place, London W1. Tel: 01 636 2237.
and at: 6 Stephens Mews, London W1. Tel: 01 636 8492.
Sell nine different blends, in a variety of roasts: Mountain, a high grown coffee; Westminster, a Kenya blend; Mayfair; Savoy, a Mocha blend; Criterion, a Brazilian blend; Piccadilly; Household, an American blend; Austrian, with roast figs added in the Viennese style; Coffee and Chicory and Turkish. All can be supplied by post (minimum order 3 lbs.) ground to your own specifications or unground.

MOORE BROS. LTD.

171/2 Sloane Street, London SW1X 8QG. Tel: 01 235 5145;
and branches at: 66 Notting Hill Gate, London W11 3HT. Tel: 01 229 5347; 248 Fulham Road, London SW10 9NA. Tel: 01 352 8466.
A variety of blends available to personal shoppers and mail order customers: Breakfast No. 3 blend, Belgian Roast, East African, Special Mocha, Pure Brazilian, Italian Roast, Choicest Old Mocha, Mysore and Mocha Blend, Costa Rica, Finest Colombian, Choicest Kenya, Monaco, Matured Old Java and Light and Dark blend.

DRURY TEA AND COFFEE COMPANY LTD.

Mepham Street, London SE1 8SH. Tel: 01 928 2551.
Sell (and will post to mail order customers) a variety of their own blends, in varying roasts: Breakfast blend, After Dinner blend, Moka d'Or, Viennese, Coffee and Chicory and Espresso.

TEA

R. Whittard

Tea is still the most popular of all our national beverages, accounting for about 70 per cent of all our non-alcoholic drinks. It is the least expensive. With a minimum of 200 cups to the pound, even at as much as £1.00 per lb., that is only ½p per cup. Tired, it stimulates; shocked, it soothes; discouraged, it comforts; in hot weather, it cools; in cold, it warms; always, it refreshes.

Teas should be available in great variety to suit everyone's preferences. But nowadays most teas sold in the UK are the standard blends and tea bags, made up from mixtures of India, Ceylon and Africa teas in varying proportions, some of which are very good, marketed by the leading companies, Brooke Bond, Lyons-Tetley, Typhoo, the Co-op, etc. Up to fifty years ago, every food grocer prided himself on being a tea-blender, and would supply blends, made up to his customers' individual requirements, from original teas which he himself had carefully tasted and bought. This speciality trade has now dwindled to about 5 per cent of the market and is catered for by the fairly wide variety offered by the older firms of Twinings of the Strand, Ridgways, Jackson's of Piccadilly, and Melrose's of Edinburgh, whose blends are available throughout the country from most good grocers. In addition, there is a small number of specialist firms, which are prepared to supply, either by mail order or in their shops (see list at end), original and particular teas not available elsewhere, but worthy of the attention of connoisseurs.

The characteristics of such teas are briefly:

Darjeeling, Indian. A seasonal tea from the Himalayas, greatly prized for its Muscat flavour. In short supply and expensive. The second 'flush' is considered best for flavour, but always the larger-leaved 'Orange Pekoes' have better flavour than the smaller-leaved 'Brokens', which, however, are richer and stronger.

Assam, Indian. Strong, rich, heavy teas, with some astringency. Seasonal, and the earlier pluckings have a pleasant, mellow flavour. In all grades, from the very best to poor. The best quality leaves, which have been manufactured in the old orthodox way, have a blaze of golden tip, and this is the traditional Irish tea which stood on the hob all day long without becoming bitter.

Dooars, Indian. Much softer and more mellow teas than the Assams, with a full, rich liquor with deep colour.

Nilgiri, Indian. The best qualities have good flavour, with a bright liquor, not unlike Ceylons.

Ceylon, Sri Lanka. The highest grown are best for quality and a flavour, reminiscent of lemon, varying according to season from light and delicate to strong and pungent. The teas grown at lower levels vary in richness and colour, with a softer, more mellow flavour. The less astringent are good for serving with a twist, or very thin slice, of lemon, and also for making iced tea. Some shops in the UK will stock Ceylon teas from certain districts: Nuwara Eliya and Dimbula Districts are thought to produce the best qualities and flavour, Uva District gives a richer, heavier tea, and Kandy a fuller, stronger and more coloured tea.

Kenya, African. Kenya teas have improved tremendously over the past twenty-five years, and the best have good pungent flavour, comparing favourably with good Ceylon teas.

Lapsang Souchong, China. A distinctive smoky or tarry flavoured tea. Usually thin in the cup, but very pleasant drunk neat, or used for mixing with other teas, a very little adding aroma and taste. The flavour is strong and a little goes a long way. In recent years it has become difficult to obtain from China, and more is coming from Taiwan as a result. The latter is stronger in flavour, but much coarser, with usually a smaller, more stalky, and less black leaf than the genuine China.

Keemun, China. A rich, soft tea, fragrant and delicately flavoured, with little or no astringency. The smaller-leaved Keemuns have better quality and more fullness than the larger-leaved, and should be more expensive. All should try Keemuns, which have no harsh character and are really refreshing.

Jasmine, from China or Taiwan. Usually available as a large leaf tea with flowers, and/or as a small leaf tea (scented orange pekoe). Jasmine tea has a delightful flavour and delicate fragrance. It is expensive, but very little is needed to produce that pleasant flavour, or to add a distinctive character to other teas. It should not, of course, be used with milk, lemon or sugar, which drown the flavour.

Formosa Oolong, from Taiwan. Semi-fermented teas, with a pungent and distinctive flavour, but little or no colour in the cup. An acquired taste, which is either liked or disliked at once, but well worth trying. Lower priced ones have more colour, but the best qualities, though light, have greater astringency, and should be used neat or for mixing with other teas.

Green Teas, from China or Taiwan. Non-fermented teas, usually 'gunpowders', but sometimes Chunmees are also available. Little or no colour in the cup, but quite strong and astringent. In the dry leaf, a loosely made open leaf will be the less astringent, and will be good for making mint tea in the North African style. The neat, tightly rolled leaf will, however, be the better quality, with a brisker liquor in the cup and also the more refreshing drunk neat during a rich meal.

Earl Grey Mixture. One of the earliest of speciality blends, from a receipt given by Earl Grey to Jackson's of Piccadilly in the nineteenth century, and which most firms in the trade now try to imitate. It is usually made up now from good quality Darjeeling and China teas, and is artificially scented to a greater or lesser degree with bergamot. It is a very popular and universal specialist tea, but the scent is not to everyone's taste.

Everyone has his own favourite tea, or blend of teas. But there is a vast variety of teas which have never been tried except by a select few. Be adventurous and experiment, track down the distinctive, specialist teas, be brave and taste them; mix different ones together and make up the blend of your own choice for your own enjoyment. One hundred years ago the Victorians had their closely guarded tea caddies filled with two or three different grades which they mixed according to their mood; why not emulate them and recapture some of their gracious living? In any case, always buy the best quality of the type you prefer, remembering that tea is not expensive.

After finding the tea you really like, there are some basic rules to obtain the perfect cup. First, it must be stored in a dry place in an airtight container and away from all strong smelling substances. Freshly drawn water should be used, and, as soon as it comes to the boil, added to the tea in a heated tea-pot. The usual measure is one teaspoonful per person, and one for the pot, but should be according to taste. Strongly flavoured teas, such as Jasmine or Lapsang Souchong, will not need too much. Larger-leaved teas will require a full five minutes for infusion, smaller-leaved and fannings less. Stir before pouring. Make a little ceremony of the process, and you will be enjoying a nectar fit for the gods.

SOURCES OF SUPPLY

ROBERT JACKSON LTD.

171 Piccadilly, London W1V 0LL. Tel: 01 493 1033; and branches at:

6a Sloane Street, London SW1;

1 Basil Street, London SW1X 9LE;

24 Kendal Street, Hyde Park, London W2 2AE;

37-41 Seamoor Road, Bournemouth, Hampshire;

37 Ephraim, Tunbridge Wells, Kent;

Thos. Oakley, 9 George Street, St. Albans, Herts.;

Halsey and Sons, Market Place, Hitchin, Herts.

Jackson's teas have a very special place in the world of English tea drinkers, and are probably the best-known of all the 'speciality' teas. Their various blends and 'originals' are available from the various branches of Jackson's, listed above, and can also be supplied mail order from the main London branch. Choose from Earl Grey, English Breakfast, Ceylon Orange Pekoe, Darjeeling, Coronation Tea, Jasmine Blossom, Lady Londonderry's Mixture, Lapsang Souchong, Formosa Oolong, Ching Wo, Assam Flowery Broken Orange Pekoe, Lemon Tea, and Russian Tea.

FORTNUM AND MASON

Piccadilly, London W1A 1ER. Tel: 01 734 8040.
Will supply their own blended teas to postal customers: Darjeeling, Royal Blend, Keemun, Earl Grey, Pure Ceylon, Lapsang Souchong.

WHITTARD AND CO. LTD.

111 Fulham Road, London SW3 6RP. Tel: 01 589 4261.
Sell an enormous range of teas to personal shoppers and by mail order. Of the Indian and Ceylonese teas they stock a range of Darjeelings (Orange Pekoe, Flowery OP, Golden Flowery OP, Tippy Golden FOP, Ext. Sp. Tippy Golden FOP); Ceylon Broken Orange Pekoe, Rich Broken Orange Pekoe and Superior Broken OP; Assam (medium, choice, best and pure blend); Indian fannings; Breakfast Blend and Household Blend (Nos. 1, 3 and 6); and pure Ceylon small leaf. For those who prefer China teas, there is an equally comprehensive selection: Lapsang Souchong; Keemun (in varying strengths); Green Teas (Formosa Gunpowder, Chunmee and Moyune Gunpowder); Formosa Oolong (Black Dragon, White Rose and Peach Blossom); scented teas (Jasmine, Mandarin and Rose Petal); and various blends of China teas (Drawing Room Blend, Darjeeling and Keemun blend, Pelham mixture and, of course, the ubiquitous Earl Grey).

BUYBULK LTD.

Tunnel Bank Road, Bourne, Lincs. Tel: Bourne 3291.
Sell one or two of the more specialist teas in bulk: Assam, Earl Grey, China Keemun and their own Indian and Ceylon blends. Orders can also be collected from the Buybulk warehouse.

GRAYS OF WORCESTER LTD.

Orchard Street, Worcester WR5 3DP. Tel: (0905) 352388.
Sell their own varieties of various blended teas, to mail order customers. In common with all other tea retailers, they occasionally experience difficulties in obtaining supplies of specific teas, but they try to keep stocks of the following: Ceylon Celestial blend; Earl Grey; Jasmine; Superfine (particularly suited for hard water areas); Regency blend; and Bo Gum China tea. Check with their office before ordering, as stocks cannot be guaranteed for any particular blend.

YOUNG AND SAUNDERS LTD.

5 Queensferry Street, Edinburgh EH2 4PD. Tel: 031 225 6075.
A reasonably wide variety of Indian and China teas available by mail order: Ceylon No. 1, 2 (Tips) and No. 3 (BOP); Darjeeling No. 4, No. 6, de luxe (BOP), and Twinings Darjeeling blend; Assam 'Creamy Cup' No. 4; Earl Grey (Jacksons, Twinings and Young and Saunders own blend); China Blend, Lapsang Souchong, Keemun, Jasmine and Green Tea; English Breakfast and Queen Mary blended.

CULPEPER LTD.

59 Ebury Street, London SW1W 0NZ. Tel: 01 730 0361/2; and branches at:

21 Bruton Street, Berkeley Square, London W1X 7DA;

9 Flask Walk, Hampstead, London NW3;

14 Bridewell Alley, Norwich, Norfolk.

Sell their own 'Indian Ocean Tea', a broken orange pekoe, in ¼ lb. and ½ lb. packs, by mail order and to personal shoppers at any of their branches.

MOORE BROS. LTD.

171/2 Sloane Street, London SW1X 8QG. Tel: 01 235 5145; and branches at:

66 Notting Hill Gate, London W11 3HT. Tel: 01 229 5347;

248 Fulham Road, London SW10 9NA. Tel: 01 352 8466.

A fairly wide range of teas available, both to personal shoppers and to mail order customers: Peers Blend, High Grown Ceylon, Ceylon Orange Pekoe, Choice Assam, Pure Darjeeling, Darjeeling GFOP, Lapsang Souchong, Choice Keemun, Assam and Ceylon Blend, Darjeeling and Ceylon Blend, Darjeeling and Assam Blend, Earl Grey, Silver Blossom Oolong, scented Orange Pekoe, Mandarin with Flowers, Gunpowder, Darjeeling Golden FOP, Ceylon BOP, and Assam Broken Orange Pekoe.

ALGERIAN COFFEE STORES LTD.

52 Old Compton Street, London W1V 6PB. Tel: 01 437 2480.
Despite the name, a number of teas are also available from the shop, to personal shoppers and to mail order customers: Brabo Ceylon, Keemun, Gunpowder Green Formosa, Pan Yong China, Lapsang Souchong Formosa, Darjeeling and Jasmine with Flowers (China). Minimum mail order quantity, 1 lb.

TISANES

Herbal infusions, or tisanes as they are more properly called, have become increasingly popular of late, although probably not for the 'medicinal' properties ascribed to them by health food faddists. They are easy to prepare – by quite literally infusing quantities of the herb in boiling water for five minutes or more – extremely refreshing, rather unusual and a worthy alternative to the standard 'cuppa', should you feel in the mood to experiment.

Tisanes can be obtained from the following suppliers by mail order:

CULPEPERS LTD.

21 Bruton Street, Berkeley Square, London W1X 7DA. Tel: 01 629 4559.
and at:

59 Ebury Street, London SW1X 0NZ;

9 Flask Walk, Hampstead, London NW3;

14 Bridewell Alley, Norwich. Tel: Norwich 618911.

Culpepers supply the following tisanes to personal shoppers and to mail order customers: Camomile (Belgian and German), Celery, Cowslip Flowers, Lime Blossom, Peppermint, Raspberry Leaf, Rosehip and Yerba Mate.

INFINITY FOODS

25 North Street, Brighton, Sussex.
Stock a wide range of herbs, some of which they particularly recommend for use in tisanes: Aniseed, Burdock Root, Comfrey, Chamomile, Coltsfoot, Dandelion Root, Mint, Peppermint, Rosemary, Sage, Sassafras and Verbena. All available to personal shoppers and by mail order.

ROBERT JACKSON

171 Piccadilly, London W1.
Jackson's are now selling three of the more popular herbal teas as part of their own range of more standard teas: Rosehip, Camomile and Peppermint – all available at the various Jackson branches and by post from the Piccadilly store.

WHITTARDS

111 Fulham Road, London SW3 6RP. Tel: 01 589 4261.
Sell and will post to mail order customers, the following tisanes: Verbena (lemon scented), Chamomile Flowers, Lime Tree Blossom, Vervain, Peppermint, Rubbed Mint and Golden Matte.

FURTHER READING

A Modern Herbal, Mrs. M. Grieve (Jonathan Cape)

A Taste of the Country, Pamela Westland (Elm Tree Books)

A Taste of England – The West Country, Theodore Fitzgibbon (Dent)

Beer Drinkers Companion, Frank Baillie (David and Charles)

Beers of Britain, Conal Gregory and Warren Knock (Johnston and Bacon)

Bread, Joan Wiener and Diana Collier (Robert Hale)

Cookery of England, Elizabeth Ayrton (Deutsch)

Cooking of the British Isles, Adrian Bailey (Time-Life, Inc.)

Cottage and Country Recipes, Audrey Parker (Faber)

Culpepers Herbal (Foulsham)

English Cheeses of the North, Ambrose Heath (Harrap)

English Cheeses of the South and West, John Arlott (Harrap)

Fish Cookery, Jane Grigson (Penguin)

Fish Cookery, Michael Woods (Ward Lock)

Food and Drink in Britain, C. Anne Wilson (Constable)

Game Cookery Book, Julia Drysdale (Collins)

Good Beer Guide, Michael Hardman, ed. (CAMRA)

Good Things, Jane Grigson (Penguin)

Health Food Guide, July Allen and Michael Balfour (Garnstone)

Herbs and Spices (National Federation of Women's Institutes)

Herbs for all Seasons, Rosemary Hemphill (Penguin)

Herbs for Health, Louise Evans Doole (Wittshire)

Herb Gardening, Claire Loewenfield (Faber)

Herbal Teas for Health and Pleasure (Health Science Press)

Home Baked, G. and C. Scurfield (Faber)

How to Grow and Use Herbs, Ann Bonar and Daphne McCartney (Ward Lock)

Illustrated Herbal Handbook, Juliette de Bairacli Levy (Faber)

International Wine and Food Society's Guide to Herbs, Spices and Flavourings, Tom Stobart (David and Charles)

Lakeland Cookery, Jean Seymour (Cumbria Tourist Board)

Making Chocolates, Alex Leaver (Michael Joseph)

Natural Foods Cookbook, Beatrice Trum Hunter (Faber)

Naturally Good, David and Marlena Spieler (Faber)

New Ways with Fresh Fruit and Vegetables, Pamela Dixon (Faber)

Northumberland Cookery Book (Northumberland Federation of Women's Institutes)

Northumbrian and Cumbrian Recipes, Patrica Doughy (Oriel Press)

Penguin Book of Herbs and Spices, Rosemary Hemphill (Penguin)

Recipes from Country Inns and Restaurants, Delia Smith (Ebury Press)

Recipes from an Old Farmhouse Kitchen, Alison Uttley (Faber)

Recipes of Old England, Bernard N. Bessunger (David and Charles)

Scotch, Ross Wilson (David and Charles)

Spices, Salt and Aromatics in the English Kitchen, Elizabeth David (Penguin)

Traditional English Cookery, Maggie Malpas Pearse (David and Charles)

Vegetables for the Epicure, Roy Genders (Robert Hale)

Whiskies of Scotland, J. J. S. McDowall (John Murray)

Wholefood Cookery Book, Ursula M. Cavanagh (Faber)

Wine, Hugh Johnson (Mitchell Beazley)

World Atlas of Food, Jane Grigson, ed. (Mitchell Beazley)

World Atlas of Wine, Hugh Johnson (MItchell Beazley)

Your Daily Food, Doris Grant (Faber)

USEFUL ADDRESSES

English Vineyards Association, York House, 199 Westminster Bridge Road, London SE1.

The Tea Council, Sir John Lyon House, London EC4V 3NJ.

Dairy Produce Advisory Service, Milk Marketing Board, Thames Ditton, Surrey.

North of Scotland Milk Marketing Board, Claymore House, 29 Ardconnel Terrace, Inverness IV2 3AF.

Farm and Food Society, 37 Tanza Road, London NW3 2VA.

Company of Scottish Cheesemakers, 82 Union Street, Glasgow G1 3QS.

British Farm Produce Council, Agriculture House, Knightsbridge, London SW1.

Dutch Dairy Bureau, Dutch House, 307-8 High Holborn, London WC1V 7LP.

Apple and Pear Development Council, Union House, The Pantiles, Tunbridge Wells, Kent TN4 8HF.

Market Advisor, National Federation of Women's Institutes, 39 Ecclestone Street, London SW1W 9NT.

Scotch Whisky Association, 20 Atholl Crescent, Edinburgh; and at 17 Half Moon Street, London W1.

Academy of Pure Malt Whisky, c/o William Grant and Sons Ltd., 40 Piccadilly, London W1V 9PA.

Food Education Society, 29 Golden Square, London WC1.

Soil Association, Walnut Tree Manor, Haughley, Suffolk.

Biodynamic Agricultural Association, Broome Farm, Clent, Stourbridge, Worcs.

CAMRA, 94 Victoria Street, St. Albans, Herts.

White Fish Authority, Sea Fisheries House, 10 Young Street, Edinburgh.

Herring Industry Board, 10 Young Street, Edinburgh.